SAMBA
& the Monkey Mind

SAMBA
& the Monkey Mind

Leonard Williams

W · W · NORTON & COMPANY · INC · *New York*

*To June—not because
she allows monkeys in the house,
but because she insists
that they be there.*

CONTENTS

PHOTOGRAPHS

from the author's collection
are reproduced following
pp. 34, 66

AUTHOR'S NOTE

IN English-speaking countries, *Lagothrix lagotricha* (Humboldt) are popularly known as 'woolly monkeys', a misleading name because the hair and coat of these monkeys does not in any way resemble wool. Their prominent belly gave rise to the common name by which they are known in South America: *barrigudos* (bag-bellies), a name which at least defines a true characteristic.

Although there are many species of *barrigudos*, each with distinct physical characteristics and varying in coloration from grey to brown, my own references are specifically to the grey types. The term 'woolly monkey' is retained throughout this book as being more familiar to English-speaking readers.

I am especially indebted to Dr Konrad Lorenz, Sir Kenneth Clark and Sir Julian Huxley for their valuable suggestions and help in the preparation of this book.

Passages from *King Solomon's Ring* by Konrad Lorenz and *My Friends the Baboons* by Eugène Marais are reproduced by permission of Methuen and Co. Ltd.; from *Ring of Bright Water* by Gavin Maxwell by permission of Longmans, Green.

Murrayton, Cornwall   LEONARD WILLIAMS
January 1965

PART I
The Woolly Monkey

PLAN SHOWING MONKEY SECTION OF HOUSE

CHAPTER I

Green Fingers

IF A NEIGHBOUR were to ask: 'Who was the young man I saw in your garden yesterday?' we are not likely to reply: 'A Nordic European of the genus *Homo sapiens*. He is bimanous and bipedal, and has opposable thumbs.' But since we have friends that induce some people to enquire: 'What are those black things out there in your back garden?' an explanation of some kind must be given. We say they are primates, *Lagothrix lagotricha*, of the group Ceboids. But should someone ask: 'What's the name of those lovely little black monkeys?' we reply: 'Woolly grey monkeys, from the Amazon jungles in South America.'

When people ask me why I keep monkeys, I never quite know what to say. The question embarrasses me and makes me feel that I am perhaps eccentric. But I do know when my interest in woolly monkeys began. As a young man I developed the somewhat unusual habit of visiting the zoo, not once a year on Bank Holiday Mondays, but almost every weekend throughout the year. I cannot say what gave rise to this habit, unless it was the simple fact that the happiest and most exciting days of my childhood were those spent at the zoo. It is very easy to speak of turning points in our lives, of people and events that shook our thinking or changed our hearts, without realising that an accumulation of previous events and influences had already prepared us for such changes. So true is this, we are often attracted by some things without knowing or even caring why, and such was my state of mind during those early days at the zoo. I usually went alone, for whenever I persuaded a friend to go with me my habit of remaining by one cage for a considerable time would drive my companion to despair.

There was hardly an animal at the zoo I did not know, and it was a coincidence that I happened to meet 'him' on the very day of his arrival. He had no name, unless you call *Lagothrix lagotricha* a name. The keeper could give me no other information, and seemed surprised by my interest. It was just another monkey in the monkey-house. But he was nothing of the sort; he was a woolly monkey from the Amazon jungle, and the most beautiful monkey I had ever seen. His eyes were magnificently expressive, and he was sad, and he sobbed, as woollies do when you whisper to them.

*   *   *

There is a special beauty about the woolly monkeys that is hard to name. In repose they are contemplative, serene and plaintive, as though Nature had chosen them to look sad on her account. In many ways they are more human-like than other monkeys. With their dark, soulful eyes, they look like little Negro philosophers.

Woolly monkeys are found in most parts of tropical America, ranging from southern Venezuela, through Brazil, Ecuador and Peru. The main feature that distinguishes them from the Old World monkeys is the prehensile tail. This tail has a pad-like underside at its end, from six to seven inches long, the texture of which is not unlike that of kid leather. It is a most beautiful and remarkable organ, and is often referred to as a hand-tail. Woolly monkeys can hang by this tail alone, and for long periods. They also use it for picking up, carrying and reaching out for objects that are beyond the range of their arms, in much the same way as an elephant uses his trunk. Almost everything the elephant can do with his trunk the woolly monkey can manage with his tail. Even with an object as difficult to hold as a ball, the end of this sensitive tail somehow manages to curl itself round it and grasp it as firmly and securely as any hand; and when the owner moves along, up goes the tail in the air as though it had a life of its own and was resigned to going wherever the rest of the monkey chose to take it.

When you have lived a long time with woolly monkeys you feel such respect for the prehensile tail that you begin to regard it as a separate personality. Sometimes Samba will climb on to my lap and lean back, lazily and contentedly, her arms and legs sprawled out, as she sinks dreamily into a pensive mood. There she sits, utterly relaxed, her arms outstretched and her back resting against me, peering across her fat belly at her feet and— that tail! Is *he* pensive? Not a bit! He is about to start a merry little game of his own. He rolls up his prehensile tip into a neat little curl and makes a sideways jump and back again. Samba watches with mild interest. He draws himself up, so slowly, moves a little from side to side, and then, quite suddenly, flops down on to my hand. He, too, has another side to his nature, and after a hard day's work in the garden, swinging, hanging, twisting and turning, he wants to enjoy an idle moment no less than Samba. Shall we stroke him, or tease him? We move our hand away and allow it to fall on top of him, tit for tat. He follows suit immediately. Now he moves up again and over to Samba, hovering in front of her face. Suddenly, she grabs him with both hands as though catching a fly, and laughs in the way that woollies do, with a 'huh, huh, huh' and a great shaking of the head. A dog will play with his tail, but here it seems the tail plays with the monkey. There are very few of Samba's moods in which her tail does not play an important part.

The strength of the prehensile tail is quite staggering. If the fully-grown male in a fit of rage throws it round your neck you will be savaged almost to death before you can be free of it. When the male attacks he will some-times use his tail like a whip, a thirty-two-inch whip with a diameter of over two inches, that lashes you in the face until you are black and blue. And attached to this tail is a body of incalculable strength that can weigh as much as thirty pounds, with four long and sinewy limbs to use against you. Each limb has a devil's hand on the end of it, and while two of these hands dig and tear at your eyes and face, the other two and the tail will fasten on to your arms so that you can barely move them in order to defend yourself. Added to all this fighting machinery is a mouth more dangerous than that of the lynx; not because of the long canines that protrude over its lower jaw and their interlocking action when they bite and drag, but because of the cunning of the primate brain that drives them into your skull, your face or your throat. This brain knows what it is doing, and those powerful fingers are gouging your eyes because a blind opponent is easier to kill.

In the early days we had three monkeys: Liz, Samba, and Lulu. No one in this country had been successful in establishing a breeding pair, though there had been two woolly monkeys stillborn at Molly Badham's zoo in Staffordshire. We wanted to discover whether the special environment we had built for our monkeys would be suitable for mating, and Molly Badham was kind enough to let us have one of her mature males for this purpose. That is how Pepi, at the age of six, came to join our woolly monkey community as a husband for Lulu, the most mature of the females.

I therefore set out to achieve a special relationship with Pepi, one that would allow me to continue my friendship with Lulu in the event of her having a baby. All went well for the first year, during which time Pepi had married Lulu and made it clear that she belonged to him and no one else. The honeymoon went on for months, it fact it never stopped. In that year, like most married men, Pepi put on weight, but it was the weight of more sinew and muscle and of the development from adolescence to manhood. His shoulders broadened, his forearms thickened, his canines grew, and at the age of seven, when he weighed twenty-five pounds, the mere sight of him was enough to raise a doubt in my mind. But we continued to be friends, and everything pointed to the fact that he still trusted and respected me.

When I take my mind back to that terrible day, I often wonder whether, had I not turned my back on Pepi and knelt down to pick up a bucket from the floor, the attack would have been made. I remember that, as I turned, he was lying on a high shelf by the window, looking quite relaxed, and that Lulu was in the outside enclosure. Then it happened: no warning, no sound, just a heavy weight that fell on my shoulders, a great tail that went round my neck, two long legs pinning my sides, two powerful arms wrapped round my head and face, and a strange pressure on my skull.

When you are standing and an animal attacks from the front you stand a chance, even a good chance if you keep your wits about you. But what can you do when a twenty-five-pound death machine wraps itself round your neck and your shoulders, and there you are, crouching on the ground, with a bucket in one hand and a cigarette in the other? I did nothing, absolutely nothing, while I counted, very slowly, up to ten. Pepi also did nothing. You can do a lot of thinking in ten seconds, and besides trembling with fear and working out the best plan of counter-attack and escape I was thinking about such niceties as main arteries, the jugular vein, and damaged eyes. I also thought about my wife and my children, and those docile, affectionate little friends of ours—the little woolly people!

Ten seconds are up, so I talk to Pepi. 'Hello, old man. There's a good Pepi. Huh, huh, huh! How about a game?' He does nothing. How long do I have to remain sitting here, just waiting—five minutes, ten? (As a zoo-keeper, I had been in trouble before, trapped in a hippo den. There was one way in, and the daylight went out as two ton of hippopotamus appeared in the entrance. That was another time when I counted up to ten, and said my prayers as well, only then the hippo came right in, looked straight at me, turned round and walked out again.) Still, Pepi has done nothing serious as yet, and I can hardly sit here all day, so let's try standing up, very slowly. Not bad, a little more pressure from the tail, but nothing to worry about. Now for a different tactic—be masterful! 'Off, Pepi!' Pepi tightens his hold and champs his jaws.

And then my nerve broke. I lifted my arms with the object of beating him off, when he seemed to leap away from me. What a stroke of luck! I made for the door, but he came at me across the ground. There was not enough time to open the door, so I turned and kicked him, full in the face. It was a foolish thing to do, because even in play woolly monkeys will always grasp whatever is thrust at them: feet, hands, brooms, anything. They just hang on, and it is extremely difficult to shake them off. But I was lucky, for the kick connected, and though it made little impression on him, it gave me the few seconds I needed to get out of the room and lock the door.

I was in no pain, and I began to congratulate myself on a miraculous escape, when I saw my hand. I could not believe my eyes, for it was torn across from near the centre of the palm. My eyes felt wet, and also my face and neck. Blood was pouring down from the top of my head, over my face and on to my clothes. So that was why Pepi had leapt away from me! With two highly successful drag bites, administered at lightning speed, he had decided to jump clear and prepare himself for the next stage of the fight. I was not only unaware of the fact that Pepi had bitten me, I had experienced no pain whatever.

No longer under the nervous strain of directing all my energy and alertness to coping with Pepi's attack, I was now able to take stock of what had really happened, and as I stood there, contemplating with horror the injury to my hand, a terrible pain began to creep into it. I will spare the reader the details of my recovery, and record simply that I was in fact an extremely fortunate man to escape with a scalp wound that required ten stitches, and a lacerated right hand. Although it was six months before I could use my hand again in my professional work as a guitarist, today it is as good as ever for playing. I am only reminded of the scar on my head on those futile occasions when I optimistically use a comb; it is time I took the advice of the *luthier*, Harald Petersen, who is always telling me I should use a duster.

Several months passed before I recovered from the injuries received from Pepi, and during this period I was unable to attend to him personally. I could not bear the thought of sending him to a conventional zoo, where the conditions would be so different to those he had known with us, but I could not take the risk of allowing another member of the family to attend to him. Fortunately the Paignton zoo in Devon was willing to give Pepi the largest enclosure in the primate section, and so came that sad day when a badly damaged and disillusioned monkey-crank watched one of his friends taken away to a new home.

Lulu did not appear to be distressed by the separation, so we tried to find another mate for Pepi, without success. As the months passed Pepi fell into a decline and Lulu had to be returned to him. That was nearly three years ago, and today, as I write, both monkeys are happy and well.

*　　*　　*

In retrospect, I suppose that I had to make the mistake that most monkey-lovers make at least once in their lives, of hoping that with me it would be different. We think that perhaps we have 'green fingers' with animals, or even that our fingers may be greener than most, regardless of the fact that all fingers are the same colour when they are bitten, and that all hands look alike when there is a finger missing.

Men are dangerous when they are in love, so how could I bear ill will towards Pepi? If anyone tried hard to tolerate the impossible, Pepi did. Battles between rival males in the woolly monkey community are terrifying to see. Yet here was a 'wild man' making concessions, torn between his deepest instincts and respect for his keeper, for Pepi was no coward and was never afraid of me. I could hold him down with a neck strangle-hold, applying all my strength to prevent him from escaping, and he would bare his great canines and chuckle with glee. In these rough games (all games with monkeys are rough) I was often hurt, but never seriously. A large piece of my cheek would be twisted as though it were Plasticine, and teeth would sink into flesh to a point painful to bear.

But there were never more than a few bruises and red marks to show at the end of it. Pepi took his punishment like a Trojan, even when he went too far and received a blow from me that spun him round like a top. When playtime was over, Pepi was never a problem. If necessary I could pick him up bodily and carry him, as one would a child, back to the monkey-room.

By attempting such a relationship with Pepi, I was defying the lessons of my own experiences and those of others who had attempted similar experiments. Here was a fully mature male, healthy and virile, not reared by me from babyhood, and so possessive about Lulu that even the wild birds in the garden were not allowed to hop too close to her. Yet I would enter the inside monkey-room, with Lulu there, and turn my back on him, or I would go straight up to him while he was guarding Lulu, hold out my arms, and say: 'Poor old Pepi, I don't want your Lulu', and he would wrap his enormous tail round his own neck, bury his face in his arms, and shake with emotion while I consoled him, with Lulu still sitting there only a few feet away. Sometimes he would spring at me, throw his arms, legs and tail round me, sob with emotion, and as mark of the conflict he felt, of fear struggling with affection, urinate on me. I knew that I was challenging a million years of instinct with an affection acquired in a single life-time, but I believed that the attack, if it came at all, would occur in precisely this situation, with Pepi clinging to me in his fear and seeking reassurance. Indeed I was convinced that if I continued to tolerate his emotional outbursts and made no advances to Lulu, he would be inhibited, disarmed and unlikely to attack. All I had to do was to stand there and console him, and in time he would learn to trust me.

In the light of Pepi's attack, my theory would seem to be proved false. Pepi, however, was an exceptionally aggressive male compared with other male monkeys I have known. In the chapter entitled 'Character and Dominance' I have defined what I believe to be two different character-types of woolly monkey, and I am not yet convinced that my experiment would fail with a male of the Samba type—a physical type that is more intelligent and less aggressive. Considering that Pepi came to me at the age of six, a mature and semi-wild animal, and also that he belonged to the more primitive character-type, his tolerance of my intrusion into his private life was indeed remarkable. I shall certainly try again with another male when we have built our new woolly monkey sanctuary in the country, and when we have found a suitable male for Samba. And next time I shall act with more caution and with greater understanding.

CHAPTER 2

'Other Sheep Have I . . .'

FOR EVERY BABY monkey captured in the Amazon jungles a mother loses her life. The method of capture is to shoot the mother, and when she falls to the ground dead take the baby, if still alive, from her back. Torn from a natural environment where they would remain with their mothers and be nourished by them for as long as fifteen months, these four-month-old babies are packed in small crates and sent on a journey of thousands of miles. Many die on the way, and those who do survive arrive at the airport half dead or in a very poor state of health.

Almost every case known to me of private owners who have endeavoured to rear these baby monkeys has followed the same tragic pattern, a struggle of life and death; yet they are the only ones who stand a reasonable chance of regaining health and reaching adulthood. The mature and healthy woolly monkey that one occasionally sees at the zoo has nearly always been presented by someone who reared it with all the comforts of a home and garden and on a superior and more comprehensive diet.

The importance of a substitute mother for a baby woolly monkey is made clear in a letter we received from a Mrs Rex. The extract here explains how she came by her woolly monkey Samba, the very same Samba who belongs to us today, for Mrs Rex died two years ago and left Samba to our care: 'I received a letter from an animal

importer to say he had a tiny baby woolly for sale, so I
went to see it . . . There in a huge cage, crouched in the
corner in the sawdust, with its tail covering its tiny face,
was the smallest monkey I have ever seen, looking cold
and sad, no hair on her tail, and very little elsewhere. I
lifted her out and she looked at me and said a very weak
"eelk!" and tried to crawl under my coat. I *had* to take
her home with me . . . I made a little hammock and
suspended it round my neck under my jumper (it was
November) and there baby Samba lived and thrived, for
she was too young to leave her mother. Day by day she
gained a little, her hair grew, and she got cheeky with my
dogs, and at long last she climbed a rope up to the ceiling!'

So Samba lived, and today at the age of five she is one
of the loveliest female woolly monkeys you ever saw. She
and Liz are the greatest of friends, and will end their days
here; both indeed may well outlive the author.

Woolly monkeys are not so delicate as some 'authori-
ties' would have us believe. They are highly emotional
and responsive and become sick and dejected under
average zoo conditions. With fresh air, plenty of space,
swings, ropes, play material, and free access at all times
to warm inside quarters, they will thrive under the most
severe climatic conditions and changes.

When young monkeys are healthy, they are extremely
tough. Little Jimmy, eighteen months old and weighing
only seven pounds, once fell from the top beam of the outside cage, flat on his middle. It was his own fault, for he
had been trying to outwit Liz, who is older and stronger.
Overcome with the satisfaction of getting home one good

nip and making Liz squeal, Jimmy had taken a flying leap
at her while she was hanging by the tail from the top beam.
He missed, which is something I would not have thought
possible for a woolly monkey, for whatever else he is doing,
especially in high places, that tail is always there, an-
chored to something. We had sown new grass seed in the
garden enclosure, and Jimmy fell thirteen feet on to hard
earth. He lay on the ground, hardly moving, and croaked
for several minutes. By the time I had reached him he was
on all fours, with a strong list to starboard and his head
twisted to one side. He crawled along like a broken insect.
Then he stopped and was violently sick. I was so distressed
and sorry for him that it was only by the greatest effort of
will that I could leave him unattended for a while, this
being the best way of observing the extent of his injuries.
Quite suddenly he sat down and began to look more com-
fortable. A second later, he started to climb the pole,
slowly at first, then faster as he neared the top. As Liz approached, he shook his head and sobbed, and they huddled
close together. The huddle developed into 'huh, huh, huh'
and then into 'aaarrk', and the game was on again.

A little while later, when the game was over and
resolved, Jimmy settled down to a meal of rice pudding,
half a lettuce, and two pieces of malt-bread and butter. He
then looked up at me, and said 'eelk', which is woolly
monkey language for 'Hello! I'm feeling fine', and I
thought of Charlie Chaplin, who, above all artists, has
shown us that we need more than the will to live, we need
the will to be cheerful about it—come what may.

*　　　*　　　*

Our woolly monkeys—Liz, Samba, Pepi, Lulu, and Jimmy—all reached adulthood, and today they enjoy perfect health. Liz and Lulu both had enteritis when they were eighteen months old, and both recovered without the use of antibiotics. Veterinary officers in zoos consider enteritis to be generally fatal for woolly monkeys; even with antibiotic treatment, recovery is rare.

What chance would a human infant have of surviving enteritis if it were simply pumped with antibiotics and left alone in a cage to care for itself, with no attention of any kind? I have seen baby woolly monkeys in the dealers' shops, huddled up in corners, covered with diarrhoea and cage filth, cold, sick and close to death. I have stood there, watching their pathetic and human-like faces, knowing that all would die whether purchased or not, unless a Mrs Rex came along to rescue one of them. I have bent down close to the cage, whispering 'eelk' and 'huh, huh', and watched their faces light up as they answered with a tiny 'eelk' and came crawling over towards me. What a great day of rejoicing it would be, if these little babies were to find their way back to their mothers!

When Lulu was sick with enteritis she was nursed at night by my wife and myself in our own bed. During the first week of her illness her weight fell from twelve to seven pounds. During the day she rested in a portable cot which we put close to a heater in our kitchen. We tempted her with delicacies and allowed her to have anything she wanted. Within a few days she took a little orange juice, a few grapes and a small piece of bread and butter. In two weeks she was well enough to rejoin the monkey community. Liz was also taken sick, and recovered under the same treatment. None of our monkeys has been sick since that time, nearly four years ago.

In captivity, woolly monkeys are not very intelligent about what they eat, except that they will have nothing to do with food soiled by excreta or urine. Given the opportunity, they are likely to eat poisonous plants native to this country and such harmful substances as oil paint and cement. Since their diet in captivity is so different from the one provided by their natural environment, this is understandable. Attempts to make good the deficiencies of a natural diet with vitamins or vitamin-charged foodstuffs are either bad for the animal or unnecessary. To give vitamins to a woolly monkey when it is not even provided with eggs, butter, cheese, and rice is ludicrous. They will adjust themselves and thrive on a varied diet of almost every vegetable (but no onions), fruit, malt-bread and butter, cocoa, eggs, cheese, rice, and meat. They also like to gnaw small chop-bones, and are far too intelligent to come to any harm with bone splinters.

Until successful breeding lines have been established in this country, I am in principle against having the woolly monkey as a pet; but if you are unable to wait until that happy day arrives, then at least make sure you get a female, and remember that you will have to give it almost as much care and attention as you would a human baby, just as Mrs Rex did with Samba.

I would like to end this chapter with a tribute to Mrs Rex. It is sad to think that she died without knowing that in her many letters to us she had written a very important piece of woolly monkey history. Perhaps one day I shall be given the opportunity of publishing these letters, for they represent a treasure trove of old-world reflections on the wild life that surrounded her little house in Weeley Heath, Essex, where she lived with her many animal friends, her flowers, her books, her memories and the spectacles that Samba was always breaking. The extracts that follow are taken from her last letter to us:

'When Samba was still quite a baby, Tail seemed to be a separate entity. Often she would sit with a toy in her hand, and Tail would creep over her shoulder and snatch the toy, much to Samba's dismay! It was a long time before she was able to relate cause to effect.

'It is wonderful to come home from shopping and hear a little voice say "eelk". When I open the door two little arms go round my neck and a sweet little black suede face presses against mine. With squeaks and sobs and a great shaking of the head, she says: "What a long, long time you have been away!" And then the dogs greet me, and Raffles the parrot says "Allo, allo", and I am home. Samba is such a dear, and sometimes I think that when Christ said: "Other sheep have I that are not of this flock", he meant these funny little woolly people, who cheer us so much.

'The grass was so long this spring, my mower would not cut it, so I answered an advertisement in the local paper for a woman gardener. She made a very good job of it, and when I took out a tray of tea for her, Samba came trotting along with me. Samba didn't like the sound of the motor-scythe, and was completely terrified of *her*. She had a very red and shiny face, a hat with a pheasant's feather, which wobbled all the time, a very short checked and patched coat, and under the coat a pair of enormous buttocks—looking just like the oldest inhabitant's prize marrows at the chapel sale. She also had shorts, men's socks and black boots. In a deep, deep voice, she turned to Samba and said: "Allo". Samba looked at her with her eyes popping out, and with a shrill scream rushed up my skirt and vanished under my jumper. She was really stiff with terror, and I was at a loss to know how to get her over it.

'Every time I now start my own mower I can hear Samba scream in her room, and when I go in to console her, there she is, hunched in a corner, shaking and shivering, and it takes all day to wear off. Even then we have to go all round the garden, into every shed, upstairs and under the beds, in the cupboards and wardrobes, before Samba will believe *she* is not here! And if I cut the grass in the evening when Samba is asleep, her first thought in the morning is to rush to each window and glare into the garden in search of *her*.

'Today the crocus and violets were out wide to the sun, and even a few daffodils, so I went for a walk in the lane with Samba and the dogs, and met the vicar of a neighbouring parish. He stopped me and said: "I don't know how you can bear to have that *thing* crawling on you." I was much taken back, for I am a quiet person and inclined to peace, but I said: "Vicar, the same God who made you made Samba as well, and I am sure He loves us all." My own vicar loves Samba, and when he leaves after one of his parochial visits I am never quite sure to whom the visit was paid! But then that vicar *is* a man of God.'

CHAPTER 3

Eelk!

'WHERE'S YOUR teddy, Samba?' Samba replies with a joyful, high-pitched 'eelk'. She goes to the cupboard, opens the door and rummages through a collection of playthings belonging to the children until teddy is found. He is then hoisted on to her shoulders and held there while she walks round the room in an upright position. Or she will bring teddy to you and curl up with him in your lap, making little sobbing sounds and chattering with her teeth as though overcome with emotion.

'Eelk' and the sobbing and teeth-chattering ritual are allied with many moods, and have roots that lie deep in the sexual instincts. With a human being an infinite variety of moods and emotions is given a distinctive and expressive form, but with a woolly monkey one mood will often merge with another, leading to a whole sequence of moods. The end may be in domination, submission, reconciliation, or sexual consummation; or it can stop short of any one of these.

The following situation will illustrate this. Samba has just been threatened with the cane for jumping on the piano and not getting down when she was told. She climbs on to my lap and sobs, seeking consolation and the reassurance that I will not punish her. As I caress her, her mood changes, and the sobbing sounds give way to the short intakes of breath that express the sexual drive.

Or let us say that Liz is in trouble with Samba, who, incidentally, is the boss. Liz has probably made the great mistake of helping herself to some grapes without Samba's permission. Samba has crept up behind and delivered a small but decidedly unpleasant nip on Liz's rear. Liz screams with rage, but Samba nonchalantly turns her back and proceeds to eat the grapes as though Liz were not there. Liz is now inconsolable. She has been bitten and she is not going to get any grapes. When I appear on the scene she jumps on to my back, curls herself round my neck and sobs, with the forearm shielding her eyes, manifesting all the same signs of affection for me as Samba does for her teddy. I now approach Samba, who is well aware of my intentions and tries to make off with the grapes. I grab her by the tail and give her a few smart whacks, whereupon she screams, drops the grapes, and collapses into my arms in the sobbing ritual. Liz, during Samba's punishment, has become almost delirious with satisfaction, evidenced by the woolly monkey's special war-cry, 'nyonk, nyonk, nyonk'. But with Samba sobbing her penitence she quickly follows suit, and I am left standing there, embraced by two grief-stricken females.

Life continues, but peace does not stay for long. Liz and Samba are now becoming sensual, and if I allow this to continue we shall be back where we started, with another war on our hands. As the dominant male in this drama, I am expected to choose between Liz and Samba, and the only way out of this dilemma is for me to produce more grapes. Liz and Samba are delighted with the change in the programme and respond with a chorus of 'eelks'. I don't admit for one moment that this proves my sex-appeal is unable to compete with a grape. I think 'eelk' in this context is monkey logic for 'first things first', i.e. one can always make love, but one cannot always get grapes.

In an emergency woolly monkeys can usually be dispersed if one imitates the quiet cough-like grunt of the jaguar. This will send them running away and up to the highest place they can reach. But it is an unkind thing to do. They huddle together upon the topmost beams, their little black faces frozen in fear, making their danger call, 'yook, yook, yook'. One should resort to the jaguar cough only if the situation is serious, though I doubt whether it would have made any impression on Pepi at the time of his attack on me.

The richest part of monkey language is expressed not by sounds but by movements and gestures, as is so of most animals. When Samba has discovered a new toy and she is not quite sure whether it is alive or not, she will grasp it with the end of her tail, come running to me and jump on to my lap. There she will sit, waving the toy up and down with her tail for both of us to investigate, looking at me every so often to see what I am going to do. If I am un-co-operative, she will drop the toy in my lap, and, if this fails, she will push my hand towards it. When I pick it up and show that it is safe to handle, she will then say 'eelk' to indicate that she is satisfied with the reassurance. When I was in Australia I had a golden-crested cockatoo named Gerry, who would bring a ball to me by pushing it across the floor with his beak. When the ball was at my feet Gerry would stand there, swaying from side to side and inviting me to a game with a rhythmic thrusting back and forth of the head. Only when the game started did Gerry squawk with excitement and delight. Here we have a situation that is parallel with Samba and the toy horse. Both Gerry and Samba displayed a higher faculty of expression by movement and gesture than they could have achieved by sound. The sounds in monkey language that express elemental and instinctive feelings are nevertheless rich and varied in meaning, and it is interesting and important to interpret as many of them as we can.

The most common sound is unquestionably 'eelk'. In the most general terms it means 'all is well'. There are many kinds of 'eelk', most of them sharp, high-pitched and joyful, with variations in pitch, inflexion, and strength, but they all stem from 'all is well'. For example, Liz is curled up in the top bunk, half asleep, and Samba is having a midnight snack on the shelf over by the window, for she likes to look at the stars while she eats her last orange for the night. Samba, for no apparent reason, unless it has just occurred to her that life is wonderful, says 'eelk'. Liz, whom we thought asleep, replies 'eelk' so quickly as to sound like an echo. Translated this would mean: Samba: 'I'm feeling fine.' Liz: 'So am I.' Or we might see Liz swinging by her tail in the far corner of the garden enclosure, by the apple tree. She hears Samba 'eelk' some forty feet away, over by the hatch which enters the monkey-room, and she answers with a loud and long 'eeeoo . . .' that begins as a crescendo and falls with a trill-like glissando into '. . . ooolk'. It is a most beautiful sound and in character and strength resembles the woolly

1 Garden enclosure

2 Runway connecting with the monkey-room indoors

3 Liz and Samba in the monkey-room

4 On the shelf over the monkey-room radiator

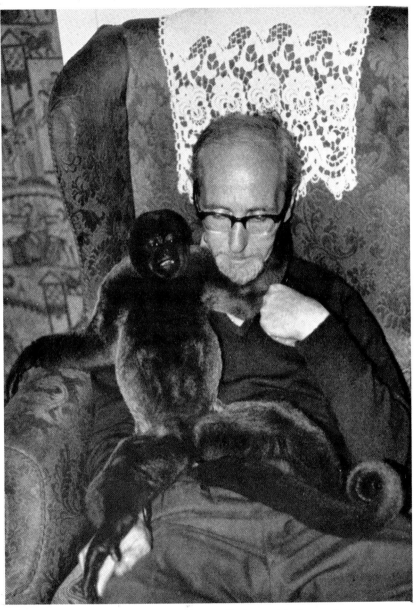

5 '. . . *here it would seem the tail plays with the monkey*'

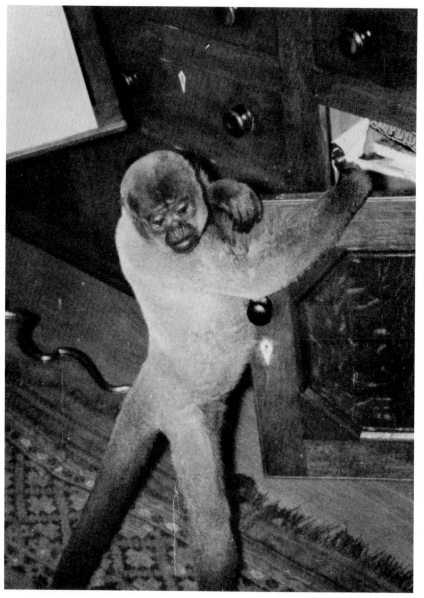

6 Liz uses her tail like a tripod

7 Jimmy

8 Jimmy's favourite television programme

9 Asleep in the sun

10–12 Jimmy and Max

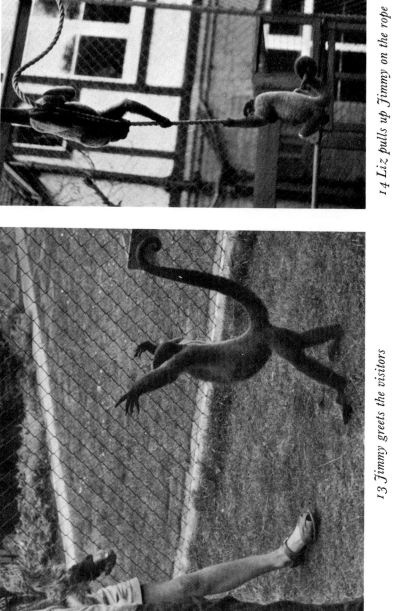

13 Jimmy greets the visitors

14 Liz pulls up Jimmy on the rope

15 Samba and her teddy

16–19 The chair game

20 In this unusual photograph Samba assumes the posture of the female woolly monkey making sexual overtures

22 *Liz says hello*

21 *In-fighting*

23 Samba helps herself

24 Samba sobs

25 'If you want to know what is behind the play-bite of a monkey
you must bite back . . .'

26–27 '. . . . but for the fact that he believes her to be a human
dwarf he would have eaten her long ago'

monkey's call-cry. There can be little doubt that 'eelk' is
one of many signal sounds meaning 'all is safe and well'.
'Eeeooolk' means that things are going particularly well.

One of the most intriguing sounds in woolly monkey
language is 'nyonk, nyonk, nyonk'. It is carried on very
much in the style of Morse code, and is an exceedingly
difficult sound to interpret. In a free-for-all with 'nyonks'
coming from all directions, it often means somebody is
getting the worst of it, and that what began as one against
one, or two against two, has developed into three against
one. But one cannot rely on this interpretation. If I stage
a mock battle with my wife, June, and she pretends that
I am hurting her, Samba will put a restraining hand on
me, or sometimes in her confusion on June, adopting a
protective attitude and 'nyonking' almost continuously.
And when peace is restored Samba plays her part in the
reconciliation with the sobbing ritual. A protective or
defensive attitude is unusual for a monkey, except when
the male is guarding his mate or the mother her baby. As
in human beings, loyalty in a monkey is an acquired
characteristic, something that has to be learned, and in
the realms of slave-like devotion the honours must go to
man's eternal friend, the dog.

'Yook, yook' means danger, fear. If 'eelk' is 'yes', then
'yook' is 'no'. When woolly monkeys are frightened,
whether by unfamiliar sounds in the night, shadows, reflections in the glass or moonlight, it requires only one to
start for the others to join in. This 'yooking' will often
continue long after the cause of the disturbance has
ceased. Fortunately for us this rarely happens, for when

it does it is usually at night, and one of us has to get out of bed and go into the monkey-room to console and reassure them. This I do with a number of my own 'eelks', which I am not very good at since I have difficulty in pitching my voice to anything like their register; but it usually works, and when it fails there is always the titbit or a cup of tea.

The call-cry of the woolly monkey must be one of the most beautiful sounds in the whole of nature. It is a sustained, deep-throated but high-pitched trill, and can only be likened to the sound of one hundred canaries in unison. You are not likely to hear it except where there is enough space and distance to justify its use, though Samba will sometimes trill when she hears children laughing and playing in the street.

A champing of the teeth, with saliva falling from the mouth, and much jumping up and down, is nothing much to worry about in the case of the female woolly. If you see it in a male, run for your life.

'Huh, huh, huh' is a good-hearted chuckle, accompanied by rough and tumble, pinches, twists, bites, squeaks, and squeals, with no ill-feeling and no special object in mind. Gouging at eyes and pulling out handfuls of hair must all be taken in the proper spirit as part of the game.

'Aarrk' is explosive, similar to the swift and short jerk of a rattle. It usually occurs in real horse-play, when the female holds on fast and allows and even invites you to apply a number of hard play-bites and pinches. The motto of this game seems to be: 'Please bite me hard so that I can bite you harder!' Her ecstasy is spiced with just a touch of fear, but if you stop she is capable of shoving her foot right into your mouth and demanding more, with a heap of 'huh, huh, huhs' to prove she means it. If you are foolish enough to comply, the 'aarrks' will develop into 'aaaarrrrk', and if you push on beyond this you will soon be in a situation that only a male woolly monkey can resolve!

The real measure of Samba's intelligence is shown by her understanding of our language. If she fails to comply with my commands, it is always out of disobedience or because she is too preoccupied to pay attention, but the quickness and accuracy with which she complies when she wants to, show that she fully understands their meaning. The following phrases can be said in a variety of inflexions and tones. They can be made forcefully or casually, or even whispered, and they can be spoken by anyone, though this does not mean she will respond to orders that are unreasonable.

'Take me for a walk.' Samba will take you by the hand and conduct you on a tour of the room, or of the whole house if you permit her.

'Don't tail the chair.' This is when Samba is out for a game and has gripped the leg or rail of a chair with her tail and is about to pull it over with a crash to the floor. She always releases the tail-hold when given this order. She also obeys 'No tail!'

'You'll get the stick', or just 'Stick'. This deterrent works nine times out of ten.

'No biting.' Her understanding of this is remarkable,

because 'no' acquires an absolute meaning for most animals in the course of their training. If I give this order to Liz, who may be biting a book she has picked up, she will drop the book and turn her attention to something else. But Samba distinguishes 'no' from 'no biting'. If I say 'no', the book will be placed on the floor. If I say 'no biting', she will stop biting but continue to occupy herself with the book, turning it over in her hands and opening the pages.

'Be careful!' Samba has finished her tea and is placing the cup perilously near the edge of the table. Her hand is making tentative movements and she is concentrating hard. I shout 'Be careful' so that she will manœuvre the cup into a safe position. If it just balances, the operation is considered a success.

'Jump on Max!' Our Alsatian does not like this, but Samba usually obliges, with plenty of 'huh, huhs' and sometimes a 'nyonk' or two.

'Go to June.' Samba knows everyone in the family by name, and will usually comply, but it is unreasonable to give such requests the force of an order unless it is important. For a dog an order is an honour and a pleasure to obey, but never for a monkey.

Samba is familiar with many more phrases as well as variants of the ones I have recorded. The following are selected from these and I record them without comment: 'Want to dance?', 'Take off my glasses', 'Want to swing?', 'Would you like a cup of tea?', 'Jump', 'Don't open the door', 'Don't go in the kitchen', 'Come back in here', 'Don't go in the lounge', 'Stay in the kitchen',

'Stay in the lounge', 'Don't go in the hall', 'Get off', 'Time to go, goodbye', 'Come on, back to the monkey-room', 'Where's your hat?' One can substitute 'yes', and 'yes, you can' for all the 'don'ts' that appear in the fore-going phrases and Samba will respond accordingly.

Samba can lift a cup and drink from it almost as skil-fully as a chimpanzee and replace it on the table slowly and carefully so as to avoid spilling or dropping the cup. She can unscrew the lid from any jar and remove the con-tents, turn any kind of door-handle and open the door, and will allow her face and hands to be washed when they are sticky with fruit or jam. During the evenings she spends with us in the lounge she can hold her urine for as long as three hours, which is quite unusual for a monkey. Her habits of cleanliness are her own idea and it is easy to see when she is restless and wants to go back to the monkey-room. She can push a go-cart around, sit in it while you give her a ride, or pull it along with her tail. She will look at television with a sustained and concentrated interest for as long as ten minutes, saying 'eelk' with great excite-ment to any animal that appears on the screen, particu-larly a dog or monkey. She trusts us when we swing her round and round by the tail, even when she has no hold of her own and her safety depends on us. She never bears a grudge when she receives a hiding for being particularly naughty, such as when she bites Max too hard or tries to twist off his ear.

Max is completely fooled by Samba's sub-human appearance and intelligence. He regards her as a very small and black-faced human being, and would no more think of biting her than he would any other member of the family. He is too noble to be afraid, and when Samba cheats he will sometimes come over to me with an expression that seems to say: 'Why *does* she play so rough?' Samba is often hard pressed when the game becomes wild, especially when her head disappears by accident inside Max's mouth. When she gets over-excited and really sets about him, the poor chap is disconcerted and doesn't know what to do. During these tussles, Samba draws upon the woolly monkey's whole repertoire of bad language, with squeaks, 'nyonks', and 'aarrks', but Max is not allowed to bite, bark, or even growl. These are Samba's terms, and if they are unacceptable to Max he must retire defeated. But for the fact that he believes her to be a human dwarf, he would have eaten her long ago.

CHAPTER 4

Monkeys in the Amazon

THE EARLY literature on animal life in the Amazon regions contains very little information on the behaviour of South American monkeys. The naturalists Wallace and Bates confined their travels mainly to the rivers, making short saunters along the banks in search of butterflies. When we consider the forbidding character and density of the neotropical forests, we can sympathise with some of the Victorian naturalists in their reluctance to penetrate more than a few feet into the jungle itself. As for observing the arboreal monkeys who live there, on the jungle roof, the explorer Paul Fountain remarks: 'It is extremely difficult to learn about the habitat of monkeys in a vast and dense forest where most of the trees are 150 feet high. If five are seen, possibly there are fifty more out of sight. All the monkeys are shy, and if watched remain still. They are lively and noisy, but avoid showing themselves. I have heard them near my camp for days together without seeing one. Only by concealing oneself and watching patiently can a glimpse of them be obtained.'[1]

There are many descriptions of pet monkeys who have attached themselves to the camps, and descriptions of dead monkeys, especially those seen roasting in preparation for the traveller's lunch. Wallace writes: 'We caught a glimpse of some monkeys skipping about among the trees, leaping from branch to branch, and passing from one tree to another with the greatest ease. At last one approached too near for its safety. Mr Leavens fired, and it fell, the rest making off with all possible speed. Having often heard how good monkey was, I took it home, and had it cut up and fried for breakfast: there was about as much of it as a fowl, and the meat something resembled rabbit, without any very peculiar or unpleasant flavour. Another new dish was the Cotia or Agouti, a little animal . . .'² (A great deal of Wallace's reporting reads like a recipe book.)

Almost every book on the early expeditions to the Amazon contains similar accounts of how to roast monkeys and what they taste like, which are rather disconcerting for one in search of information on the habits of live animals. But not all the Victorian naturalists were like Wallace. Paul Marcoy, who travelled through the Amazon region in 1860, refused to eat monkeys because they reminded him of children. He writes: 'A large and black woolly monkey that was tied to the prow of the boat, broke his cord and sprang upon me at a single bound. He threw his long arms around my neck and I had every prospect of being strangled. I struck him on the nose and tried to free myself from his embrace, when I already felt that his arms were beginning to relax. I saw his teeth chatter, and noticed a deep look of poignant sorrow in his eyes, and I was immediately ashamed of having struck that grandfather of humanity. To make what amends I could for my disgraceful act, I kissed him on his black muzzle.'³

Among the many stories that have been told by hunters, there is one in particular which has often been disputed,

but which I am convinced is true. It is said of neotropical monkeys that if a young one is abandoned by its
mother in the panic of flight, the first female that passes
will take it on her back and continue running. I believe
this because of Samba's habit of grasping her teddy-bear
when she is alarmed and taking it with her on her back to
a position of safety. She is never so frightened as to take
flight, but often some unexpected and unfamiliar sound
will cause her to run a short distance and climb to some
high point in the room, usually the mantelpiece or the
top of the piano, and when she does she will invariably go
out of her way to capture her teddy first.

Very little is known about the feeding habits of woolly
monkeys in the wild. Observers have reported prehensile-
tailed monkeys as eating large insects, and even young
birds and eggs, but no one seems to be sure. Our monkeys
are expert at catching moths, and they will eat cater-
pillars. The speed of their hand movements and the ease
with which they capture a moth or a butterfly in flight is a
most impressive sight. They are fond of meat, and they
will sometimes augment it by chewing at the frayed end
of a rope, just as some dogs (chows, German shepherds,
and huskies in particular) will chew and eat the carpet if
they are incorrectly fed on lean meat with no fur. (A real
dog should be fed as though it were a wolf, and occasionally given a complete rabbit or hare.) Omnivorous animals require roughage as well as protein, and woolly
monkeys are no exception to the rule. They are also
extremely fond of eggs, and there can be little doubt that
they plunder the nests of birds in their own habitat.

Our monkeys also eat a little soil which is easily obtained from their outside enclosure. I have no confirmation as to whether they do this in their own habitat, though it is well known that many omnivorous mammals do. It is possible that certain chemicals in the earth neutralise the acid juices in the stomach. The habit of earth-eating is practised by many of the Indian tribes in the Amazon.

It is generally known that most monkeys live to a great age. There was a capuchin on my round at the Melbourne zoo who was forty-two years old at the time I left in 1951. At the London zoo a woolly monkey by the name of 'Chips' (presented to the zoo at the age of fourteen) lived until he was eighteen; though perhaps I should say he *survived* in prison and without a mate until he was eighteen. As I write, Molly Badham has an old patriarchal male woolly at her zoo in Hints, Staffordshire, who is over twenty years old and still going strong. If we ignore the hazards of jungle life, of disease and predatory animals, I think we can say quite safely that woolly monkeys have a life-span of twenty to twenty-five years.

I have found the published literature on the specialised organs of the woolly monkeys and the method of woolly monkey movement too generalised and vague to have any real value. Before presenting my own observations and conclusions on this subject, a brief comment must be made on the unique character of the vegetation and geography of the Amazon jungles.

*   *   *

The geography of the Amazon region is continually

being changed by floods and storms. Even the great rivers shift their channels. Giant trees measuring up to two hundred feet high and ten feet in diameter are uprooted by winds and floods. Whole forests that have reached full maturity disappear owing to the action of rivers, and sections of forests several hundred yards in length have been seen to slide, with a great roaring sound, into the deep and swift-running waters of the Maranon and the Orinoco. Islands ten miles long, covered in dense jungle and teeming with reptiles, birds, and mammals, appear where none existed a year before.

Small birds and lizards are trapped in huge spider nets that sometimes envelop whole trees. A star performer among the poisonous bird-catching spiders is the *mygale*, which can measure seven inches across. Among a rich variety of poisonous ants, flies and hornets, the *isango*, a minute blood-feeding insect, commands a special respect among the Indian tribes.

When the railroad was being built from San Antonio to Esperanza Falls, every inch of the line had to advance through almost impenetrable vegetation. Immense trees cut through at the base remained erect and held in place by the network of vines that tied their tops to everything within a radius of fifty feet. Craig, the chief engineer on this project, wrote: 'The density of the forests was such that not even the native Indians could move ten feet without cutting their way through the web of vines; some thorny, others sticky and greasy, and all alive with biting red and black ants of all sizes. These made life one continuous torture. Punctures from palm leaves which lay face down, with myriads of needles standing erect, caused infection and permanent sores. The blow of an axe on a tree trunk would make it rain ants on us by the thousand from the foliage above. The bites of the large black ants caused a terrible swelling.'[4]

In this great continental sea of vegetation that has become known as the 'Green Hell' it is easy to see why the activity of monkeys and other small mammals is confined almost entirely to the roof of the jungle. The perils of the jungle floor make tree life a condition of survival. For the arboreal monkeys that live there the law of life must be: stay off the ground.

But life in the trees is by no means free of danger, for there are tree-climbing snakes and predatory eagles, and jaguars have been seen pursuing monkeys in the trees at a height of more than thirty feet from the ground. Paul Fountain writes: 'Monkeys seldom perceive the approach of their main enemies, the poisonous tree snakes and the jaguar. It is not only colour or similarity to some other object that enables the snake and the jaguar to approach their victims, but silent cunning and craft. The monkey sees not, knows not, until the death-dealing paw pins him down, or the darting head of the snake has struck.'[5]

The explorer Thomas Belt writes of an encounter between a monkey and an eagle. The monkey had been heard crying in the forest for more than two hours, and on investigation both predator and prey were found facing each other on the same branch of the tree. Had the monkey turned its back the eagle would have seized it. The monkey, however, kept its face to the eagle, which did not care to attack in this position. How this particular contest would have been resolved was never known, for the eagle was fired at and frightened away.[6]

It is easy to see why woolly monkeys in captivity are readily disturbed by all manner of domestic sounds—the rattling of knives and forks in the kitchen drawer, clock chimes, the scraping of a knife on concrete, even the clattering of the handle of a bucket. In the interior of the swamp forests of the Amazon, the animal and bird sounds are like nothing on earth: howls, clicks, roars, and the shrill screams of eagles and hawks.

*   *   *

With this picture of the Amazon in mind, we are in a position to consider some of the important features of primate evolution in the Amazon, and also the physical characteristics of the monkeys who have survived in it.

It is generally accepted that man and many other land mammals crossed the Bering Strait during the Pleistocene period, when there was a land bridge connecting east and west in the northern hemisphere. When the early primates went south to the neotropical forests they evolved into 'five-handed' climbers, brachiators, 'clingers' and tail-swingers. The atrophied thumb and the hand-tail are therefore reciprocal features in the evolution of neotropical monkeys as a whole, and in order to understand this relation we will consider first the anatomy and the function of the prehensile tail.

The comparative body- and tail-lengths of some of our woolly monkeys are shown in the following table:

	Head and body	Tail
Samba:	17 inches	25 inches
Lulu:	17 inches	26 inches
Liz:	18 inches	27½ inches
Pepi:	23 inches	33 inches

Specimens quoted in *Mammals of Amazonia*:[7]

	Head and body	Tail
(A) Average:	450 mm (18 inches)	680 mm (27 inches)
(B) Largest in collection:	705 mm (28 inches)	1,200 mm (47 inches)

It will be seen that the tail-length of the largest specimen (B) is double that of the body, if we allow five inches
for the head and neck. With the spider monkey, the
largest of the neotropical primates, the tail-length is normally double that of the body-length. Imagine the
strength there must be in a tail that is nearly four feet in
length and five inches in diameter at its base! To take
Pepi as our example, the tail tapers down rather suddenly
from four inches at the base to three inches, maintaining
this girth for approximately sixteen inches and then
tapering consistently from here to its tip. The immense
girth of the tail at the base is well illustrated in the photograph of Samba (Ill. 41). These facts are important for
a proper understanding of the nature of the movement
of the woolly monkey in running, walking, climbing,
holding, gripping, hanging, clinging on, and leaping.

The photograph of Samba on her ropes in the monkey-
room (Ill. 28) shows a characteristic attitude of woolly
monkeys when they are suspended with nothing between
them and the ground below, and the risk of injury from

falling is increased. The possibility of falling is remote. The point is that woolly monkeys are less experienced in falling or dropping on to level ground than most Old World monkeys. When they do, they have no 'landing' technique. A baboon, for example, can jump several feet to level ground with some of the skill that we find in the cat, and even the rhesus monkey is an expert 'lander' compared with the woolly monkey. When woolly monkeys are venturesome and allow themselves to drop four or five feet from a hanging position to the ground, they usually land on all fours in a most ungainly and amateur fashion. One could say that they are inexpert at falling or dropping to the ground because they are so expert at not falling! That is why a woolly monkey could never be knocked or pushed off the branch of a tree. It would have to be scraped off. Hunters in the Amazon have in fact shot them and found them still hanging by the tail when they are dead. Even in death, it seems, the instinct to stay in the trees lives on. How difficult it must be for a predatory eagle to capture even a young and small woolly monkey! A woolly monkey attacked will only take to flight when the likelihood of escape is almost certain. If there is the slightest doubt, it will cling on and face the enemy. This is characteristic of all our monkeys in their play activity. The anatomy of the woolly monkey is ideally suited for clinging and wrapping itself round an object. When any of our adult monkeys do this during play they cannot be dislodged. It might be possible to detach them if one were to apply all one's strength, but only at the risk of injuring the animal.

Woolly monkeys are comparatively hopeless at fighting on ground level, unless they get hold of their opponent. To watch little Jimmy playing with a fox terrier in an open space is truly comical. When they come to grips Jimmy gives a very good account of himself, but should he turn and run, God help him. If the fox terrier is stupid enough to be a good sportsman (a term that is utterly without meaning for a monkey), he will arrive at the point the monkey is making for in time to turn round and have a good scratch before Jimmy gets there.

Woolly monkeys can and do brachiate (a hand-over-hand movement), but the tail is in constant use no matter what form of movement they adopt. Brachiating is not always the best form of movement in close canopy jungle. In no other jungle is there such a prolific growth of vine as in the Amazon, or so much vegetation that is decomposing and ready to break with the weight of an arboreal animal, even near the roof of the jungle. The instinct for tree security is so strong in the Amazon monkeys that all five 'hands' will be fully employed even in positions of complete safety, only a few feet above ground. This is well illustrated by Samba in Ill. 29.

When woolly monkeys brachiate, it is always with the added security (not necessarily support) of the tail. Even when it is not being used with specific advantage, it will add its security to whatever is going on. If you carry a woolly monkey for a walk round the garden, the tail will always be wrapped around you. The woolly monkey will hang by one arm, like the gibbon, but you will never find the tail hanging or waving about in space as though it were a superfluous organ, an impression one often has when watching the long-tailed monkeys of the Old World.

Woolly monkeys never hang by the tail alone unless the supporting branch has proved strong enough to take the weight. When they are satisfied, from long experience, that a particular branch or beam is secure, they will perform a number of amusing tricks in the tail-hanging position. They will also swing on a long and isolated rope, but not until the rope has been tested. Suspend a new rope from a great height, and see how tentatively they approach and investigate before climbing or swinging on it. Our monkeys will allow any member of our family to pick them up and swing them round by the tail, but I would never allow a friend to do this, so fearful am I of losing the monkey's confidence should there be an accident. A woolly monkey, strangely enough, has little or no objection to having its tail held, but immediately a stranger attempts to lift him by it he will leap up and grab the offending arm.

There is another species-preserving function of the tail of particular interest, one that I have seen illustrated in a natural as well as a domestic situation. When Samba is in doubt she investigates first with her tail. In the garden I have often oberved her occupied with some strange new object, a staghorn beetle, say, or a toad. Standing on two legs with her back to the toad, while peering round for a complete view, she advances cautiously and tests its reaction by a whisper of a touch with the tip of her tail. When there is no response from the innocent toad, the tail becomes more venturesome, turning it over and prodding it to see whether it bites. If it moves, Samba will jump up and down with excitement and uncertainty. As her confidence increases the toad is man-handled, until it has to be rescued from certain death.

The logic of Samba's approach to the toad is clear: she does not want to lose the tip of her tail, but it is, nevertheless, the least vulnerable part of her body. Her method of investigation also keeps her body twenty-five inches away from possible danger, and leaves her hands, feet, and mouth free for action. The same ritual is performed in the house when she is confronted with a strange object. On one occasion she disliked and therefore 'yooked' at a toy giraffe that was on the floor in an upright position. We were fortunate in having the camera ready and were able to obtain photographs of the two main stages of the incident (Ill. 40; 41). It was a repeat performance of the encounter with the toad, only this time she also acted the part of toreador by grabbing a cloth-cover that happened to be near by and throwing it over the giraffe. This would seem to be an approach to the stage of a tool-using primate. The technique of combining the use of the tail with a large palm-leaf could be very effective for dealing with small and unwelcome visitors in the Amazon trees.

I have indicated that the main function of the hand-tail is for hanging, gripping, and clinging, as well as for general movement; it is now important to relate this to the woolly monkey's atrophied thumb, for the atrophied thumb and the prehensile tail must be recognised as reciprocal features in the evolution of hand-tailed neotropical monkeys as a whole.

In swinging slowly through dense foliage, the thumb obviously becomes a hindrance. It is less of a hindrance for fast and complete brachiators, like the gibbon, but even the gibbon, compared with the anthropoid ape, has a relatively small thumb that is set well back in the hand, away from the other fingers. In their own habitat woolly monkeys spend a great deal of time simply hanging. They are 'hooked' in the trees as it were, a situation in which the developed opposable thumb is less advantageous than an atrophied thumb which functions like the little or fourth finger. Now a tree-dweller, with or without tail, does not advance through the tree backwards, nor does he advance forwards with his feet! Neither does a monkey brachiate upside down with his feet; at least, not outside a circus. In full or partial brachiating, the feet bring up the rear, so that the opposable thumbs of the feet are ready for a secure grip in any upright or semi-upright position that may be necessary. The opposable foot-thumb therefore (or great toe if you insist), far from being an impediment to moving or grasping, becomes a decided advantage for any movement that is non-brachiating.

And so we find, logically, that the foot-thumb of the woolly monkey is extremely well developed, even *more opposable* than the thumb of the human hand, and well separated from the other fingers. If the foot-hand of a woolly monkey were enlarged to the size of the human hand, it would stretch nearly two octaves on the keyboard of a piano. I have been careful to say, if the *foot-hand* were enlarged, for woolly monkeys have enormous hands and fingers in relation to their size; if the *monkey* were enlarged to the same size as a human being, its foot-hand would be able to stretch at least two and a half octaves, or approximately sixteen inches!

The hand-thumbs of the woolly monkey are usually described as being 'well-developed'. This is misleading. It is true that of all the neotropical hand-tailed monkeys the species with the least atrophied hand-thumbs are the capuchin and the woolly monkey, but compared with the well-developed and opposable hand-thumb of the Old World monkeys, such as the Indian rhesus, that of the woolly monkey is poorly developed and, moreover, is not even opposable. The atrophied thumb has the appearance of a fourth or little finger, but has less power and flexibility. When a woolly monkey picks up objects with the hand (remembering that it frequently uses the tail or the feet for picking up) the thumb moves in the same direction as the other fingers. When Samba unscrews a lid from a jar or applies herself to any action which requires twisting or turning she will often use her feet, for the foot-thumb is opposable and well developed, as it is with the orang-utan, who is also four-handed. Expressing it in common language, the hand-thumb in the evolution of South American primates is 'on its way out'.

We have seen that an accompanying characteristic of the hand-tail is a less developed opposable thumb (as in the case of the capuchin), or an atrophied thumb (as with the woolly monkey), or no thumb at all (as with most spider monkeys). And it is precisely where the thumb is most atrophied, where it is reduced to a mere stub or where it is entirely absent, that the prehensile tail reaches its fullest and most magnificent development—in the spider monkey.

It may be argued that there are arboreal mammals in the Amazon who have managed to survive quite well with no tails, or with short half-tails like the uacaris. The point is that in the evolution of the hand-tailed primates there is a development towards the large and strong prehensile hand-tail, as found in all species in the group Ceboids, the most developed of the Amazon monkeys, as distinct from half-monkeys or Pithecoids. It is also true that there are many other mammals of lower evolutionary descent, such as the harvest mouse and the opossum, who have prehensile or part-prehensile tails, but very few of them are able to support themselves by hanging from the tail alone, and none of them can use their tails in the strict sense of 'hand-tail', or with anything approaching the technique of grasping, holding and throwing that we find in the group Ceboids. (Samba often picks up a plastic bowl and throws it at me with her tail, while she is swinging on a rope.) Their nearest rival is the kinkajou.

Although some writers seem to be hypnotised by specialised features, they forget that the use-value and function of a special organ such as the prehensile tail— wonderful though it is in its own right—has only a restricted and particular value for a given species in a given environment. Yet this has not prevented them from speculating on the value of certain specialisations, such as the hand-tail, had they become universally adopted. I sometimes think that the gorilla would have become a greater object of interest for them had it been blessed with inverted nipples.

Nature is not quite so foolish as to have evolved an organ as intricate and sensitive and of such tremendous strength and size relative to the rest of the animal as the hand-tail, unless the survival of the animal in a given environment depended upon it. When we take the broader view—of the evolution of primates from monkeys through the apes to man—the tail itself can only be seen as a hindrance. It would be no less of an embarrassment for the chimpanzee than it would be for a primate concert guitarist, and God knows what kind of tail would be necessary to support a gorilla. Conversely, only the Old World provides the necessary conditions for the full evolution of primates—from half-monkeys, monkeys, baboons, gibbons, anthropoid apes, to mankind. The ground-living patas monkeys of Africa, to take an extreme example, are found in the open savannahs and grasslands. They run and walk almost with the gait of dogs, moving on the flats of their hands and feet.

Many of the Old World monkeys not only are good climbers and well adapted to arboreal life, but can move on the ground much faster than prehensile-tailed monkeys. Old World monkeys are also faster and more agile at running along branches and up and down the trunks of trees. But if the ground-living patas monkeys and the baboons of the Old World were to be dropped into the Amazon jungle they would quickly revert to an almost exclusive tree-life. And if they were able to survive for a million years or so they would probably develop prehensile tails.

The evolution of the hand-tail primates can only be understood in relation to the special problems of survival presented by the vegetation and structure of the Amazon, where *the evolution of the jungle itself follows a different pattern.* Even in the remote parts of Malaya, Sumatra and Borneo, where the jungle terrain and flora may be compared with that of the Amazon, the problems of survival are different in character.

If I were going to explore one of the habitats of the woolly monkey in the Amazon, and Samba could talk, I am sure she would give me the advice a Peruvian bush-man gave to the explorer Leonard Clark: 'White men look only ahead of them, but you must look even closer ahead, much closer!—and above, as well, and below, and on both sides, and especially behind. Never forget to look behind!'[8] And I am sure Samba would add: 'Don't forget to take your prehensile tail—above all, you will need that!'

CHAPTER 5

Character and Dominance

IN MY VIEW, a study in woolly monkey dominance must be related not only to the character of the individual monkeys, but also to different character types. In our private language at home we have always distinguished two main character types by the terms 'long-bodied silver-greys' (group I), and 'stocky dark-greys' (group II). Both groups belong to the species *lagotricha lagotricha* of the genus *Lagothrix*, and represent a variation of type within the species. In our community of six monkeys, Pepi and Liz belonged to group I, and Lulu, Jess, Jimmy and Samba to group II.

Group I monkeys—'long-bodied silver-greys'—are more aggressive and less relaxed. They are continually on the alert, with a fixed expression about the eyes of 'rhesus-like' or typically 'monkey' alertness. Their play-bites are uncontrolled and painful to bear, and by nature they are less reliable. They are less intelligent about what they eat, and will often make themselves sick from over-eating. Their faeces are usually soft in texture and highly odorous. They tend to be somewhat larger animals than the monkeys in group II.

The monkeys in group II—'stocky dark-greys'—are more amiable in disposition, more responsive to human influence, more reliable and predictable, and less aggressive. This does not mean that they are less dynamic or over-civilised; they are in fact the dominant members of the monkey community. They are more individualistic, more expressive, and as fast in movement as the others when they want to be. They move from *largo* to *presto*, whereas group I monkeys are almost always *allegro*. They are not so 'greedy' in their food habits, and their faeces are darker, firmer, and relatively odourless. The relaxed and subtle shades of expression that flicker about the eyes of the 'stocky dark-greys' remind one of the gorilla. In many ways they are like miniature gorillas.

Although these distinctions in character type are unlikely to receive zoological classification, I nevertheless believe that they are important, and I therefore ask the reader to keep them in mind.

*　　*　　*

In woolly monkey society there is female as well as male dominance. There is also a social order of rank that embraces females and males alike. The largest number of woolly monkeys we ever had at one time was six: two adult males, Pepi and Jess; two adult females, Lulu and Liz; a three-year-old female, Samba; and eighteen-months-old Jimmy. The order of rank was as follows: Jess, Pepi, Lulu, Samba, Liz, Jimmy.

Jess was a mature adult when he first joined our monkey community, and during the one year he was with us his position as ruler was assumed rather than asserted. He acted like a benevolent emperor from the moment he arrived, and his position was never disputed. It was difficult at first to explain the respect he commanded from the others, for there were many reasons why this was un-expected.

In his previous home Jess had lived as a pet, enjoying the freedom of a large garden with trees. He was five years old when he came to us, a strong, well-developed and healthy animal, who settled down in his new home quickly and happily and was friendly and affectionate with everyone. (I had hopes of him as a mate for Samba, but he died from enteritis a year later.) He displayed no sexual interest in Lulu, who had already mated with Pepi, nor in the other females, Liz and Samba. His experience of monkey communal life was nil. He did not fret for his previous master, and he was on good terms with everyone, monkeys and humans alike. Even Pepi, a stronger, larger, sexually mature animal, and highly possessive about Lulu, accepted Jess as ruler.

Jess may have been sexually immature, for most male woollies are already performing the thrusting actions of copulation at the age of three, and Jess was well into his sixth year. His sexual development may have been re-tarded from want of stimulation and example since he had lived his five years almost exclusively in human society. Perhaps he had formed a sexual attachment to his previous master, which in the parlance of behavioural science may have prevented normal imprinting, i.e. the learning of species characteristics. Whatever the explan-ation, he was not a negative or submissive animal. He had been disciplined, but his individuality and his monkey-ego were as strongly marked as those of the other monkeys.

I have a habit of working late through the night, and

many were the nights he spent with me, walking round my typewriter, waiting for the bell to ring and responding with 'eelk', helping himself to my tea, and eventually falling asleep by my side when he was tired. Sometimes he would sit up, yawn, scratch his stern, and return to the monkey-room to settle down for the night with one of his subjects. Any one of them would do: Liz, Jimmy, or even Pepi, for Lulu was not always disposed to spend the night with her master.

Samba was interested in Jess, and would often present herself to him with unmistakable intent, but Jess always treated her like a wise old man who understands but is unwilling or unable to oblige. His erections were quite imposing, though never as impressive as Pepi's, yet he never made the preliminary copulation movements I had noticed in other males who were much younger. Another extraordinary thing was that Jess played with Lulu, and Pepi did not object. Jess was the least aggressive of all the monkeys. Although a powerful animal, he was not as strong as Pepi, and he was five pounds lighter in weight. He took no special interest in Liz or Samba, both of whom were available and never shunned him. He took no special interest in any one. Why was he almost *encouraged* by the others to be the leader?

Pepi had protruding canines that overlapped and inter-locked. Jess's canines were small by comparison, and no larger than Samba's are today. I had rough games with Pepi and Jess, and I assure you that Pepi was much the stronger animal. Pepi's play-bites were unbearable for a human, unbearable for Liz and sometimes even for Lulu, but I never once heard Jess complain. Whenever I gave Jess a hard blow, for he was often deliberately naughty and seemed to enjoy the punishment, he would chuckle with glee, turn his rear end round and poke at me with his tail, just as a conscientious mother will test the baby's bathwater with her elbow to see whether it is safe.

Jess was very good at in-fighting. In a play-fight with Pepi he would always drop his head in the first attack and allow Pepi to concentrate on the back of his neck. (The thick section of muscle and bone that joins a woolly monkey's head to his back can hardly be called a neck! It is the most invulnerable part of his body.) While Pepi was thus occupied, Jess, who had grown up with a large bull terrier, would work hard at Pepi's feet, hands and tail. It was always Pepi who retired, running away, as Jimmy would run away from him, defeated and humiliated.

Pepi's fight-sounds of 'aarrk' were double the volume of Jess's, but his displays of defiance and intimidation, calculated to alarm Jess, had no effect at all. When Pepi, drooling with saliva and flashing his canines, made an awe-inspiring leap, Jess would sit there, his arms stretched out and ready, waiting for the clash that never came, for Pepi would always break his leap with a high and clumsy back-jump, and make off, careering round the garden with Jess hot on his heels.

Jess was indeed a peculiar fellow; he was also a gentleman. In his games with Liz, who is the first to complain when hurt, he never once caused her to squeal with pain. Samba and Liz were rarely seen playing with Pepi or Lulu, but they loved a game with Jess. And Jess was the only fully grown *male* monkey we ever knew who was never spiteful with children. During the first three years of his life he had been a photographer's model and gimmick, and had learned to tolerate almost anything. He should never have been a monkey.

Can you imagine five monkeys, including Pepi, all waiting patiently round the food-tray, while Jess picked out the delicacies in his own leisurely fashion? I only once saw Liz reach out and very quietly help herself while Jess was still at the tray. Jess was quite unconcerned. I know that he would not have objected had the others joined him at the meal, for by nature he was not greedy, possessive, or dominating; but he was dominant.

When Jess died, Pepi became the leader in a community of five monkeys. He was a despot. Intruders or interceptors at the food-tray were not to be thought of as he settled down to a great feast, while four peckish monkeys waited and 'yooked' their impatience. Only Lulu, his wife, was allowed to join him, and even she would sometimes wait until his lordship had finished. If Pepi was king, Lulu was queen, and not one of their subjects would approach the food-tray without permission.

Pepi was twice Lulu's weight, and, unlike Jess, he was no gentleman. But Lulu was the strongest and fastest in action of all the females, and in her play with Pepi she fought back like a tiger. Lulu was a girl who enjoyed being pursued and captured. Her problem with Pepi was to maintain a tempo of flight consistent with the thrill of escape, yet not so fast as to make it impossible for Pepi to catch her. It was like watching a weight-lifter chasing Charlie Chaplin. Of course, Pepi could never catch Lulu by his own initiative. Lulu would cover thirty feet of territory, crossing horizontal beams, sliding down poles and racing up again, while Pepi lumbered along behind, making the most impressive, giant-like leaps, but always arriving too late. The only way Lulu could make these pursuit-games interesting was to be adventurous and foolhardy. During one of her most exciting and daring leaps, I saw Pepi swing past her in the opposite direction; they both finished at opposite ends of the enclosure, Lulu seated and composed, and Pepi hanging by one arm and his tail, looking angry and bewildered.

Lulu was the finest gymnast of all our monkeys, males included. She could swing thirty feet on the end of a rope from a height of fourteen feet and back again, landing with the grace of a bird. No doubt she could have trebled the scope of this performance in the Amazon jungles. All our monkeys are good climbers, acrobats and rope swingers. Over the years the space and the equipment have always been at their disposal. But there was only one Lulu. In her, skill reached such a high level that one forgot technique and dwelt only on her art.

I have already explained how Pepi and Lulu went to the Paignton zoo. In the interval of six months before Lulu left to join Pepi, a strange event took place in our monkey community. With Pepi gone, Samba began a struggle for dominance with Lulu! Samba at this time was a little more than three years old, and Lulu was nearly five. Lulu was therefore older, stronger, bigger, more experienced, the undisputed ruler in the female hierarchy and the finest female acrobat and all-round fighter of her species I have encountered. What induced Samba to embark on what seemed an enterprise doomed to failure from the start? Samba had been with us for only one year. She was a poor climber in comparison with the other monkeys, since she had been deprived in her previous home of equipment and space. Both females belonged to the type of group II, and the social order of rank at the beginning of this new struggle for dominance was: Lulu, Samba, Liz, with Jimmy last.

Among the many encounters I witnessed during the first few months, two fights were serious. Needless to say, Samba lost both of them. In the first fight the end of her prehensile tail received a two-inch gash that took a week to mend. For several days she did a minimum of climbing, and spent most of her time sitting on the window-sill of the indoor monkey-room, looking ruefully through the glass at the others while they played outside in the sun. She spent the evenings with us in the house, keeping her tail well out of harm's way, especially when she sat down. Monkey wounds heal very quickly, and after the fourth day she began to use her tail again. During the period of recovery, life in the monkey community continued without incident. Lulu, who was never the first to begin any quarrel, behaved as though nothing had happened, and on the first day that Samba ventured into the garden enclosure greeted her with 'eelk'.

The second serious fight occurred about a month later, and I was there when it began. Samba was sitting by the hatch door of the runway that connects with the monkey-room and the garden enclosure. Lulu, returning from the enclosure, came down this runway with the object of re-entering the house through the hatch, but Samba made no attempt either to move out of the way or to pass through the hatch so that Lulu could enter. Lulu could hardly be expected to place herself at Samba's disposal, and so in her customary elegant fashion she edged past Samba, pushed up the hatch, and was about to enter, when Samba reached out and grabbed the end of her tail. Now this was sheer provocation. Lulu and some twenty-five inches of tail had already passed Samba, and it was the end of the tail that Samba grabbed before it disappeared through the hatch! It was not a play-gesture, there was no 'huh, huh', and Samba's face was inscrutable. Lulu turned and made a threatening gesture, and in seconds they were locked in battle. In all such combats, whether mild or serious, there was never any question of flight or pursuit on the part of either monkey. Samba's method of retiring was to disengage herself when she had had enough, and scream when Lulu administered the deciding bite. She would then sit back, a few feet away, examining her wounds and 'yooking', while Lulu walked off with dignity, and without visible signs of injury.

The result of the second fight was for Samba more serious. A deep tear-bite across the sole of her foot put her out of action for another week, and this time she had to walk with one foot off the ground. When the wound had healed, for many days she walked from habit on the side of the injured foot. And even months later she would lift

28–30 *The five holds of Samba*

31–35 'Behaviour studies are not possible unless the animals have enough space in which to behave!'

36–37 Atrophied hand-thumb

38 Padded section of prehensile tail

39 Footspan—opposable thumb

40 Samba throws a cloth over toy giraffe . . .

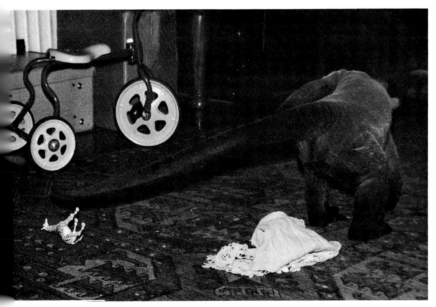

41 . . . the cloth is removed and investigation proceeds with tail

42 Teddy is rescued from strange toy dog, and cloth is picked up ready for investigation

44–46 *Tail manœuvres*

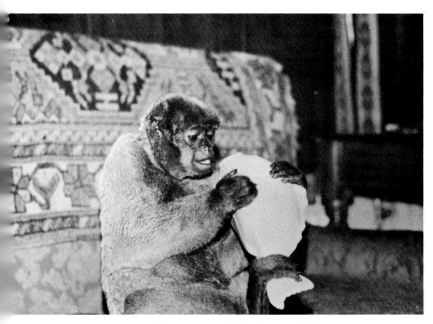

49–50 'Liz . . . beautiful, but stupid!'

51 Liz on the wheel

52 Samba with her hat on

53 '. . . she trusts me completely.'

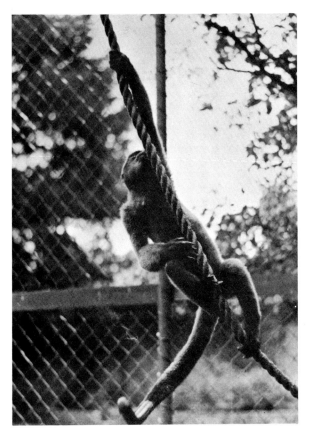

54 Django climbs his first rope in England

55 . . . and Liz brings him down

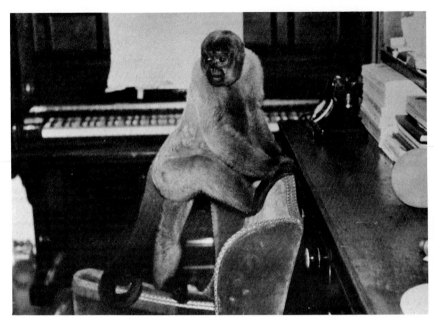

56 'Liz will have nothing to do with Max'

57 Samba and Max

58 Samba tries her teeth on one of Sam's building blocks

59 Samba and Sam

60 Max and Daniel

61 '. . . a dull evening at home'

62 Guitar trio

63 June and Liz

up her foot for inspection and for a continuation of the sympathy and consolation I gave her at the time of the injury.

I should mention here that in the intervals between their serious encounters Lulu and Samba often engaged each other in friendly 'huh, huh' play-fights. These rough games had an entirely different character, and though they were all resolved in Lulu's favour, they ended with no hard feelings on either side.

Eventually the day came when one of the minor bouts to my great astonishment seemed to end in a draw, for both monkeys sat a few feet apart 'yooking' at each other. I had never known Lulu to 'yook' before, except from fear of thunder and lightning, or at the new moon, or because a large bird unexpectedly flew across the outside enclosure with a great flapping of its wings (eagles are predators of monkeys).

During the weeks that followed, Samba gradually climbed to a position of equal status with Lulu in every aspect of life both in and outside the monkey community. It was obvious that she would have become the dominant female, but the struggle was never resolved, for Pepi in the meantime had become morose and ill at ease in the Paignton zoo, and we could not afford to delay his re-union with Lulu longer.

The perplexing thing about Samba is her persistence. Why has Liz, the largest and strongest of all the females, remained contented with her rank, the lowest in the order? Why has she never made a bid for dominance? Even little Jimmy, half the weight of Liz and with no more than one-third of her strength, is nearly her equal. And what induced Samba to persist in her rise to dominance? Outclassed by Lulu in every way from the beginning, she nevertheless continued, relentlessly, until she succeeded. Consider this simple fact: I could never hold Lulu against her will, unless I was prepared to take the consequences of serious injury to myself as well as to Lulu. She, like Liz, was incredibly strong. Samba today remains a smaller monkey than Liz or Lulu, and I can, when I choose, hold her against her will without harming her or myself. She is a strong and virile animal, but she hasn't enough strength to break a certain hold I use on monkeys when it is necessary. This hold never worked with Lulu, and it doesn't work with Liz today—even though she respects and obeys me. For this reason I can never take Liz out for a walk in the neighbourhood. If she were frightened by a car or a strange dog and in her rage made a determined effort to escape, I know I should arrive back home with both my hands in a very sorry state and with Liz nearly strangled to death. It is true that Samba, being a group II monkey, is unlikely to react in this way, but even if she did I could handle the situation without injury to either party.

Liz is always the first to squeal in a rough game, and like most squealers she is the first to break the rules. Her play-bites are exceedingly painful to bear. Watching her at play with Samba, I am forced at times to regard her as a damn fool. She asks for trouble, and when trouble comes her screams are enough to raise the dead. For all her subservience to Samba's despotic rule, they remain great friends. Together with Jimmy they often cuddle up with the mutual sobbing ritual, sleeping together at night and spending a great part of their day in fun and games. But when meal-time arrives stark realism prevails. With hands, feet, mouth and sometimes tail, Liz seizes the delicacies and makes off with them to safety, though not always successfully. A leap from Samba and a scream from Liz—and she is bereft of her ill-gotten gains. To the struggle for necessities in the monkey community must be added the struggle for luxuries.

I can only think of one explanation of the rise to dominance of Jess and Samba. It would appear that under certain conditions a younger and smaller monkey is able to convey its strength of character to the others. I do not mean in some mystical or anthropomorphic sense, but as evidenced by the power of Jess and Samba to *withstand more punishment* and by their superior intelligence. For similar reasons, Samba has been able to dominate our Alsatian, Max, whereas Liz is terrified and will have nothing to do with him. A similar comparison can be made between Jimmy and the newest arrival in our monkey community—Django, a young male who is larger and stronger than Jimmy. Django's play-bites are far stronger than Jimmy's, but Jimmy never complains. Django, however, squeals frequently, and when I have occasion to bite him (which is the most effective way of disciplining an unruly monkey) he screams with rage. When I bite Jimmy he usually laughs and bites back, and I am so demoralised I haven't the heart to find out just how hard I would have to bite in order to cause him real distress. Django is unquestionably the stronger monkey, but Jimmy is dominant, and in my opinion he will always rule Django because he is able to take more punishment.

Good-natured and courageous dogs just cannot manage monkeys. Such dogs play the game, whereas a cowardly dog, if it is big and strong enough, will kill a monkey. Samba and Jess were both quick to discover the weak spot in the character of the domesticated dog—its inbred humility. If we add to the natural shrewdness and instinct for dominance that drives the monkey-ego the superior character and intelligence of the group II monkeys, it is easy to see how Samba and Jess were able to assert their authority over animals who were much larger and stronger than themselves. Not all monkeys have enough intelligence to do this or to approach new problems (or new dogs) with caution. Samba will have nothing to do with a strange dog. She will bide her time until he proves himself to be either a coward or a sportsman. When a strange dog is brought into our house, you will always find Samba on the highest beam in the far corner of the monkey-room, well out of sight, and there she will stay until he has gone. Liz, however, will grab at the stranger through the chain-link of the outside enclosure, and scream with fright should he growl and leap up at her. But if the visitor were to stay with us for a few weeks and prove to be a real dog, a sportsman, you would be likely to find Samba pulling him along by one ear, while Liz was still screaming and poking at him as she swung from a rope beyond his reach.

CHAPTER 6

Instincts and Proverbs

'From each according to his ability, to each according to his needs' has been one of the first principles of socialist philosophy. We see it carried into effect, with slight variation, in the monkey community—when Samba eats the jam, butter and middle section of the bread, and discards the crust for Max.

It has often been said that monkeys are wasteful with their food. This is nonsense. In the first place monkeys are wasting *your* food, not theirs. Secondly, they eat and function on the basis of their own proverbs, which are altogether different to human ones. Here are four popular monkey proverbs: 1. 'Waste not stomach space on carrots when you can get grapes.' 2. 'Only a fool eats what is placed under his nose.' 3. 'Leave the worst until last; you may not want it.' 4. 'Never save for tomorrow what you can eat today.'

Unlike humans, monkeys keep to their proverbs. Let us consider, for example, proverb 1. If a cat is chewing a piece of stewing beef and you offer it a fillet of steak, it will not let the beef fall from its mouth and pounce on the fillet. There may be exceptional cats, but the cat in general will always finish what it is eating first. Monkeys, however, are never so carried away by what they are doing that they are unable to make or accept a change for the better. Only a half-wit monkey would be so foolish as to

finish an apple when confronted with grapes. Not only
will the apple be dropped unceremoniously, but whatever
is in the monkey's mouth will also be expelled.

'Only a fool eats what is placed under his nose' is
demonstrated in the following situation. When a food-
bowl is tipped up on the dining shelf in the monkey-room,
everything is turned over, examined, and selected according to preference. And if you pretend to pop something
into your mouth that they are not supposed to see, and
stand there chewing in front of them, nothing in the food-
bin will be touched. They will climb up, stare at your
mouth for some visible signs of what they are missing, and
—if you allow them to—even open your mouth, peer inside, and help themselves to whatever takes their fancy.
For a monkey what the eye can't see, the belly most certainly can miss.

'Leave the worst until last; you may not want it' is
exemplified by the contest as to who can eat the most
grapes. Monkeys are extremely logical, and the contest
therefore *begins* with who can eat the most *juice*. Each
grape will be pressed in the mouth and ejected at lightning speed with a certain amount of the flesh attached to
the discarded skin. The skins will be stripped down later,
but not if there is something else on the menu that is more
attractive.

There is no specific situation to illustrate proverb 4. It
works all the time. Monkeys do not save for a rainy day;
they have even more faith in Nature the provider than
most humans have in their insurance companies. Perhaps
the nearest Samba ever comes to having a thought for the

future is when she takes an apple to her sleeping box and puts it down beside her without attempting to eat it. This may be because she is vaguely aware that it will provide a useful snack in the middle of the night, or because she intends to eat it immediately she arrives at the sleeping box, but changes her mind when she gets there. I think the latter explanation is the more likely one.

*   *   *

Discrimination, curiosity and the desire for change are allied characteristics in monkey behaviour. Monkeys thrive on variety, and it is cruel to deprive them of it in captivity. If, for example, raisins are first preference in the daily food supply and shortcakes are last, you have only to provide a surfeit of raisins and make a drastic cut in shortcakes, and the order of preference will be reversed. Provide a surfeit of any favourite item and in time the monkey will tire of it. Reduce to a minimum or remove entirely any item which has been accepted indifferently or fitfully, such as carrot tops, and these will be greeted with enthusiasm when returned a few days later.

I am not suggesting that monkeys have no stable preference for particular foods. The most effective way of discovering what it is would be to exploit the variety factor —provide a surfeit of everything and observe the order of preference over a given period of time. Ignoring the impracticableness of this method, I am still not convinced that it would work, because monkeys are able to change their own minds and habits regardless of the laws of supply and demand, whether in the wild or in captivity.

The need for variety seems to be an integral part of higher primate psychology. It is seen in the human passion for ever-new fads and fashions, and even in the jargon of behavioural science, in which the play-activity of animals is now referred to as 'occupational therapy'. (The monkey may provide occupational therapy for you, but whatever you provide for the monkey is at best a poor substitute for his own way of life in the wild. I object to the term because it is patronising as well as pedantic.) Variety is particularly important in play-activity. It is a great day for our monkeys when I throw a large cardboard fruit-box into the monkey-room. They climb inside, fight over it, carry it to the top beams and let it crash to the ground, and finally break and tear it to ribbons. One box will keep them active and amused for an hour or more, but if a box is given to them every day they eventually lose interest. If there is nothing better to do, they will toy with it perfunctorily. But if plastic bowls, a football, rubber boots, old clothes, boxes and bundles of newspapers are each introduced at different times and for varying periods, the interest never wanes.

Our monkeys wake up in the morning very hungry, but not so hungry as to be unconcerned about where they are going to eat. In the winter months they will often bring their food from the monkey-room into our kitchen, where they can enjoy the social atmosphere of the family breakfast. On a summer's morning Jimmy can be seen carrying an apple in his tail, a banana in each hand and a lettuce in his mouth, while he hobbles with great difficulty across the monkey-room, climbs a rope, opens the hatch and passes through the runway that connects the house with the outside enclosure to settle down on the grass for his breakfast in the sun.

*   *   *

Woolly monkeys are no less cautious than they are curious. When we repainted our kitchen, the monkeys were confined to their own quarters. Normally they are free to leave by a hatch that leads into the kitchen, where they often join us, especially at meal-times. (The interior walls of our house are full of holes, with swinging hatches for the convenience of the monkeys. So far the house has remained standing.) The painting was finished in one day, and when we opened both hatches to let them through Samba peered through the kitchen hatch, took one look at the new paintwork (the colours were as before), 'yooked', slammed down the hatch and returned to the monkey-room. When I arrived in the monkey-room with the object of reassuring her, she had already left by the outside hatch (another hole in the wall) and was seated on a top beam in the garden enclosure, some forty feet away. She re-entered the house later, but it was not until the afternoon of the next day that she found enough courage to pay us a visit in the kitchen.

I have noticed that human beings who are intensely inquisitive are usually full of mistrust. Like monkeys, but without their justification, they probe and peer into everything, registering great astonishment and incredulity over the most elementary facts of life and even looking like monkeys. I think the philosopher Hegel must have had these people in mind when he said: 'It is not the business of human beings to regard new objects with the astonishment of animals.' We do not, however, expect monkeys to take things on trust; if they were not inquisitive as well as hard to convince they would have become extinct long ago. In the monkey community caution and curiosity go hand in hand, and both characteristics must be regarded as marks of high intelligence.

The innate sense of curiosity in monkeys is more closely related to their instinctive behaviour than is generally realised. We are tempted to regard a number of their play-actions as a sign of 'pure' intelligence, when the truth is that the intelligence they display in the investigation of new objects is just as much an expression of a species-preserving function as the prey-catching movements seen in the play-activity of cats. In another chapter I have argued that instincts should not be treated as though they were a blockage to new knowledge and experience, but as the ground on which new knowledge and techniques can be developed. For the present, however, I am concerned with the special character of the relation between woolly monkey curiosity and instinctive behaviour.

There are two main instinctive drives behind the monkey's investigation of a new object: is it dangerous? is it edible? Cupboards, boxes, and jars must all be opened; inside may be something very tasty, or very dangerous, or both tasty and dangerous; one never knows. The monkey's chief concern is to find out what is underneath, behind, and—most important of all—*inside*.

In the natural habitat of the woolly monkey, nuts and fruits must be opened, for the best parts are inside. The yolk lies inside the egg. Grubs are found inside holes or under the bark of trees, and they must be poked out. Large insects wear their bones on the outside; they must be pulled apart to be eaten. Dangerous spiders and insects must be rendered harmless from the inside. The monkey and the surgeon have much in common; both are dedicated to the inside, and neither is likely to be led astray by outside appearances.

Whereas the mongoose will put everything into the box, the monkey will take everything out of it. If the mongoose must take everything home, the monkey must take everything apart. Our mongoose Nicky and Jess were great friends. They would even lie together on our window-sill in the lounge, basking in the sun. When Jess was absent Nicky had no interest in his whereabouts, but Jess was never happy unless he knew where Nicky was and what she was about.

Jess's curiosity got him into a great deal of trouble. He had a habit of lifting up the cover of our divan and peering underneath to see what Nicky was doing. This was a dangerous thing to do, because a mongoose does not like to be disturbed, especially when it is in the dark and out of sight. But Nicky was good-tempered (by mongoose standards) and had learned to accept Jess's intrusions as part of a game, a game in which she was always the victor. She would run from the back of the divan round to the front, steal up behind Jess and nip him in the rear. Until I actually saw this done, I would never have believed a mongoose capable of such premeditation. It was an incredibly funny event to witness, because woolly monkeys, when they are bending down and peering, have a habit of keeping their tails high in the air. To catch a monkey unawares is one thing, but to surprise him with a nip in his most vulnerable spot is a stroke of genius. Only a mongoose could do it. The speed and the silence with which Nicky left her box under the divan and reappeared on the other side at Jess's stern constituted a miracle that Jess never really accepted. It was outside the realm of monkey possibility.

CHAPTER 7

Samba Laughs

INTELLIGENCE TESTS and the tricks of performing animals are on the whole very dull affairs, and little is to be learned from them. I believe that we can really enjoy the company of our animal friends only if we allow and encourage them to develop their own individuality. Monkeys in particular must be given the opportunity to invent and solve their own problems and to develop those skills which come naturally to them, for only in this way can their individuality be preserved.

Any kind of training which dominates the monkey-ego will only arrest the development and reduce the health and vitality of the animal. This is not to say there must be no discipline, for without discipline there can be no freedom; the undisciplined monkey is either confined to a cage or tied to the end of a chain. Intelligent animals, like children, soon learn to respect discipline, and it is my experience that the character of the monkey is actually strengthened by it.

In the early days, it was necessary to punish Samba for stealing toys from the children, but after the punishment I would always call her back to the scene of the crime, reassure her with an exaggerated display of affection, and ask the child to be kind and return the toy to Samba. In time she learned that there are ways of getting what one wants other than by taking without permission, she learned also to ask, and she learned the virtue of waiting. And whenever one of the children tried to take something away from Samba (not that they ever succeeded, for it is exceedingly difficult to take anything away from a determined monkey) she was delighted when we intervened on her side and saw to it that justice was done. This kind of treatment not only had a civilising effect on Samba, it inspired her to new heights of endeavour and monkey cunning. It did not crush her desire to be naughty, it simply encouraged her to be naughty in a more civilised and sophisticated way. She learned that if you must pinch something, then at least do it nicely and you may get away with it. Like the professional safe-breaker, Samba learned the importance of extreme care and absolute silence.

If a monkey picks up your whisky behind your back, takes a quiet sip and then puts the glass down again very carefully, how can you possibly object? But if a hooligan tears across the room, grabs a handful of porridge from your plate and spreads it from the kitchen table to the top rail of the curtains in the lounge, it is difficult to remain tolerant and placid. I can assure you this does not happen with our monkeys. I am very fond of our lounge curtains.

If our monkeys want to throw things about and tear them up, they have their own room and their own garden to do it in. They can also urinate wherever they like in their own living quarters, but not in the soundhole of my guitar. I will even tolerate an erotic christening bestowed on me from the top beam of the monkey-room when I am

not looking, because I know that this is one of the many
ways in which the female woolly monkey indicates that
she is willing. I take it as a compliment. But not on my
piano.

Animals often exhibit moods and responses similar
to those characteristic of human behaviour. The similarity
may be difficult to see, for in animals the expressions of
emotions which correspond with those of human beings
are often exaggerated or grotesque by comparison, or so
slight and fleeting in nature as to pass unnoticed. When
our woolly monkeys jump up and down with joy and
excitement, to the inexperienced observer it looks like a
war-dance; and when they are tickled under the armpit,
their laughter is often no more than a whispered 'huh,
huh, huh' with teeth bared and much head-shaking, so
that the observer begins to wonder whether they are
angry or in pain.

In his classic work *Expression of the Emotions in Man and
Animals*, Darwin was primarily concerned with the physical anatomy of the emotions, and although his study is
rich in parallels between animal and human emotional
behaviour, the emotions considered are necessarily prim-
ary and fundamental, such as those of joy, amusement,
grief, terror, and surprise. The scope for further observation and study in comparative animal and human
psychology is enormous, especially in regard to expressive
attitudes of a more subtle nature—such as those found in
evasion, sympathy, deception, shame and humility.

We are all familiar with the rogue who cannot be
demoralised, the person who puts up no defence when

caught red-handed at some trickery, who is incapable, it would seem, of sustaining a guilty conscience. Such a person was my old grandmother, who used to cheat at cards. At the end of Grandfather's reproach, even sometimes half-way through it, Grandmother would burst into laughter, and the higher he raised his voice in disapproval, the more she would laugh. With the tears streaming down her face and her enormous bosom shaking with mirth, it became increasingly difficult for Grandfather to maintain his dignity. His case simply crumbled away, and there was little else he could do but join in the fun. This was not taken in good part by other members of the family, especially by those who had lost their money. My grandmother's social technique was remarkably like Samba's behaviour in her dealings with us, as witness the following scene.

Liz is asleep on the lap of my sister Lorna, and I can just see Samba through the connecting door to our kitchen, where she is sitting on the table watching my wife June ironing the baby's napkins. Samba dislikes the iron because it hurts. In monkey logic anything that hurts spells danger, and there are only two ways of dealing with it: either go away as far as possible, or kill it, if you can. Like so many of the things which she has learned to accept in adapting herself to life with a human family, Samba knows that this strange animal, the iron, that hurts but never attacks, must be tolerated. She does not have to be an electrician to realise that nothing is to be gained by prodding, pushing, or turning the iron-animal over in order to see whether the underneath part is more vul-

nerable to attack. Watching her on this occasion, we see
her sitting on the end of the table, her eyes following the
movements of the iron, with one foot resting on the end of
the ironing board as a compromise. The scene is set
for at least a few moments of peace. This is broken by
June's voice: 'Don't touch those prunes! Now get down
and go into the lounge!' I hear the thump of padded feet
as Samba jumps from the table, and as I look up a
small, black, woolly person comes walking quietly and
sedately through the door and passes me on her way over
to Lorna. She climbs on to the settee and sits down, a
study in tranquil dignity.

A moth flutters against the window above the settee,
and Samba recognises in this a delightful and unexpected
treat. By a rapid thrust of one hand, the moth is captured;
the wings are then pulled off and it is eaten alive. With
moth-dust on her nose, she composes herself on the
window-sill, chewing rhythmically and contentedly, while
her eyes wander round the room in search of the next
adventure.

Unlike Liz and Jimmy, Samba is a diplomat and a
model of good behaviour. Where the other monkeys get
into trouble because of their innocence, Samba avoids it
by subterfuge. When Samba is occupied with something
she ought not to be doing, one rarely notices it until after
it is done.

Returning to our story, Samba is still on the window-
sill, and her roving eye has now settled on me. I am not
going to allow her to disturb Liz, who is now sitting on my
lap, so I give her a severe look and say 'No!' This causes

[83]

her to turn her head abruptly to one side and lift her chin a little in the air, which means: 'I dislike you. Go to the devil.'

She now goes into what we call her roly-poly act. This consists of describing erratic tiny circular movements in the air with her hands, and at the same time curling her tail up from behind so that she is able to hold and wiggle the end of it over her head. It is a most amusing spectacle, and though we have witnessed it countless times it still reduces us to a state of helpless laughter. It takes on quite a bizarre character when she stands up on two legs and accompanies the act with an eccentric dance, alternating the roly-poly hand movements with tentative grabs at her tail, all the while jigging up and down as though about to make a high dive from the edge of a plank. This ritualistic behaviour is usually a prelude to a high-spirited bipedal jump. It may be a long and venturesome jump, such as from the mantelpiece to a cushion on the floor, where a slight element of risk adds to the excitement. If it is a short jump, such as the one she is now contemplating from the window-sill to the settee, she will maintain her grip on the end of the tail from the moment of jumping until she lands.

This pantomime obviously expresses the pleasure Samba experiences when she jumps, but I have been unable to connect it satisfactorily with any of the instinctive behaviour characteristic of the woolly monkey. I can, however, hazard a guess: that whenever Samba is excited by the challenge of a long jump, she is also frustrated because there is no preliminary support for her tail. If she were able to grasp with her tail a branch above her head, she could swing downwards and reduce the distance of the fall, or she could hold on with one hand, lowering herself slightly before dropping. The holding of the tail above the head may be a compulsive act compensating for the feeling of insecurity. Perhaps the roly-poly hand movements express the same 'joyful frustration'—a wriggling about in space for something that isn't there. If this is the explanation, we still have to account for the fact that the bipedal jump not only is unnatural for a monkey, but invites a greater risk and is more difficult than landing on all fours. Whatever the true explanation, the whole performance is Chaplinesque in its appeal, and entirely Samba's idea. I hope that it will remain in her repertoire for many years to come.

Samba has jumped on to the settee, and is delighted with the roar of applause from her audience. She now makes her way over to the toy cupboard, and on her way walks right over Max, thus avoiding a detour of several feet in either direction. Arriving at the cupboard, she opens the door and sits down with her hands folded and resting on her knees. Gazing vacantly into the cupboard, she contemplates with total lack of interest the playthings before her. Her problem is—how to get to that cabinet way over to the left near the piano, where the sherry is? This requires great skill, perfect timing, and a profound knowledge of human instinctive behaviour patterns. She hobbles silently to the left, pivoting along on her haunches as though heavy with humility, arrives at the cabinet and opens the door with great care.

She is now faced with the most difficult problem of all: lifting a heavy sherry bottle and removing it from the shelf without touching the glasses on either side, and then doing battle with a cork that must be twisted and pulled before it will come out. Since the hand-thumbs of a woolly monkey are atrophied and of no more use than an extra little finger, she may use the opposable thumbs of her feet for a more secure grip. Fortunately it is a small cork with a serrated metal cap, a type she is able to manage on most occasions with her hands.

It is an eerie yet pleasant sensation to be seated comfortably in an armchair with one's favourite book in the quiet of Kent, to hear the tinkle of glass in a far corner of the room, and to know that over there a little black woolly poltergeist from Brazil is bent on nicking your sherry.

The cork squeaks, but there is no sound as she places it carefully on the floor. The bottle is nearly full and very heavy—infinitely more difficult to manage than a cup or a glass—and it has to be lifted up and tilted slowly. Sherry is strong stuff for the sensitive palate of a woolly monkey, and Samba is not an alcoholic; she wants only the merest nip. With the first taste, she shakes her head violently and smacks her lips with uncertain relish, because the taste both pleases and hurts at the same time. One more nip, and the bottle is placed carefully on the floor in an upright position, and 'Operation Sherry' is over. Intervention is now imperative because Liz is about to reach for it. Liz can manage to lift the bottle and drink from it, as she can from a cup or a glass, but she is clumsy and often allows the bottle to topple over when returning it to the ground.

There are now a number of courses open to me. I can show leniency—a gentle reprimand followed by a mutual drink to show that we're still good friends and that life is not based entirely on injustice, even among human beings. Or I can reflect that she has perhaps been getting a little out of hand of late. There was that incident yesterday in the kitchen when she stole an egg, and this morning she pulled the ribbon out of the typewriter. Both crimes went unpunished. She is a wonderful monkey, true, but the stick must be used *sometimes*. Tonight, however, I cannot bring myself to do it. She is sitting there looking at me in such an appealing way. I decide on method III.

Method III proceeds as follows: I stand up suddenly and dramatically, point my finger in most dominating manner, and in a loud and theatrical voice tell her what a naughty Samba she has been. I walk over and kneel down beside her on the floor, and she makes not the slightest attempt to run away. While I rant and rave, shouting in her ear, wagging my finger and telling her she ought to have the stick, a smile creeps into her eyes and the corners of her mouth. Out jumps a quiet 'huh, huh', and she leans back on her tail as my threatening finger almost taps her on the nose. She shows her gleaming white teeth, the 'huh, huh' increases in tempo and volume, the side-to-side head-shaking becomes more vigorous, until finally she laughs her head off! Samba, like my grandmother, refuses to be demoralised.

What can I do? I tell her that I love her, and that she really must not do it again. She lifts her arm and covers her eyes and sobs, her lips pursed and trembling and her teeth chattering. The other arm she puts round my neck, and I think of the words of the poet Heine: 'In the noble pattern of man He made the interesting monkey.'

PART II

The Animal–Human
Relationship

CHAPTER 8

To Humanise or Not?

ANYONE WHO HAS kept apes or monkeys will know that they have stronger individual characteristics than dogs. The similarity of the individuals in a given species varies in proportion not only to their mental development but also to their emotional level. Hippopotami, for example, resemble each other more than do monkeys, and the mental and emotional responses of the former are unquestionably lower, or if one prefers the word, simpler. Monkeys are mentally and emotionally closer to human beings, and they resemble each other less than do hippopotami. Finally, human beings are less like each other than are the individuals of any other species, and therefore, in this human way of reasoning, they are to be placed on the highest level of development.

For many people, conclusions of this nature represent a preposterous conceit on the part of the judge. The economist might point out that our 'base year' is arbitrary, and if Robert Benchley were still with us (and more's the pity that he isn't) he would probably say: 'Are you speaking from the point of view of the hippopotamus, the woolly monkey, or of man?' But if we renounce the *human* standard of measurement in our study of comparative animal behaviour and intelligence, as some philosophical analysts would like to do in their study of the human mind (hence their barren enquiry into the meaning of meaning), there is no standard left by which to measure anything; we are left with the unrelated facts—in the words of a French biologist—that a dog dogs, a rose roses, and a snail snails.

The platypus, for example, is a marsupial that lays eggs and suckles its young, but it is also an extremely primitive and specialised animal that represents an evolutionary link between reptiles and mammals, and once we admit evolutionary stages we are on speaking terms with that development and history which must ultimately embrace ourselves. The platypus, no less than any other creature, places its own accent on the unity and development of nature and life, and the fact that it is unconscious of the part it plays in the whole serves only to show that it is not responsible for the whole.

When a primate argues that primates are on the highest level of mental and emotional development, he is of course looking for trouble. But even if man is in many ways the most wretched of the animals on this planet, a little credit must be given to some men for accepting this fact and the responsibility it brings. Though I would prefer the society of my woolly monkey Samba to that of the *Homo sapiens* Verwoerd, it does not follow that I support those animal addicts who dote on comparisons expressed in the vaguest terms, such as: 'The more I see of humanity, the more I love animals.' I never heard one of them say he preferred his goldfish to Bach, his cat to Shakespeare, or his dog to a child. I make this digression with some deliberation, to show that the plea for wild-life sanctuaries, which has already become a target for satirical treatment, is just as much a plea for humanity.

There is nothing audacious in my argument for applying the human standard to animals. The conclusions I have reached are well known to naturalists; but the tendency among modern students of animal life has been to avoid the human approach in the name of scientific objectivity. Trained investigators, or behavioural scientists, as they are now called, are afraid of being charged with anthropomorphism—assigning specifically human values and sentiments to animals.

To humanise or not? If the object is to establish a mammalian hierarchy of merit, the answer must of course be 'no'. Monkeys are close relatives of human beings, and this may make them more interesting for some of us, but it does not follow that they are superior or more 'significant' than other animals. Our dog Max does most of the things one expects from an intelligent German shepherd dog. He is the second German shepherd dog we have had, and both were named Max for no other reason than that we think Max is a lovely name for a dog. We speak of Max I and Max II, but this is no mark of disrespect to their individuality. Both came from the Brittas line, and from kennels noted for temperament breeding. Max II is close in form to the original German shepherd dog, and is therefore too large to be successful as a British champion. He does not conform to the British Alsatian standard, which seems to be aiming at something like a large fox with short legs and a tendency to hip-dysplasia.

This recent and serious defect is only one in a terrible pattern of deformities that is causing alarm in the dog world. I learn that the small terrier is suffering dislocation of the lens of the eye, and that one hundred and fifty operations out of two hundred and fifty at a London animal clinic were carried out on terriers. The face and eyes of the St Bernard are dropping so low that often its eyelashes are turned inwards. A number of dachshunds are becoming paralysed as a result of spinal trouble, and toy poodles are prone to a slipping kneecap. All this is due to unscrupulous in-breeding which has its roots in the snob value of the pure thoroughbred and the demand of a fashion-ridden public for new dog models that will harmonise with the interior decoration of their houses and their cars. 'They' have also been successful in breeding goldfish with no eyes.

Our baby son Dan can take two pounds of beef straight from Max's jaws, and Max will just sit and wait, disconcertedly, true, until the meat is returned to him. Max is a family dog, and any member of the family is allowed to take this liberty with him. The claim that German shepherd dogs are by nature one-man dogs is, in my opinion, quite untrue. A number of our friends who have small dogs regard with horror the liberties our children take with Max, and it is useless to explain that it is no more dangerous than taking food from a human mouth. Indeed, I once saw an infant grab at some food that was already on its way into the father's mouth. The father protested with a spontaneous grunt that was half-way to a growl, before he was able to adjust himself to the role of an indulgent parent.

Max is not a coward and he is not a fool. He rushes up to strangers with a great bark and makes a thorough investigation before they are allowed to approach any further. Once they have met with his approval and he has received our assurance, he will tolerate them, but a little time is needed before he will accept them as friends. He is a beautiful animal with a brave heart and a wonderful nature, but though he is an individual in his own right he nevertheless resembles the other Max far more than Liz resembles Samba.

Individuality in the apes is so marked that one is almost forced to treat them as though they were backward or primitive human beings. Yet this attitude enables one to learn more about their inner life than if one examines them on the basis of a restricted animal psychology which recognises only instinctive drives peculiar to the amoral world of the animal.

It is interesting to see how important the human approach to animals is for primitive man, for whom a profound zoological knowledge is necessary in his struggle to survive. There are many primitive songs about monkeys and apes, some of which describe their habits with an exactitude that comes from the observation of the hunter. The following song gives the precise names of the trees frequented by the ape, the fruits he eats, a description of his movements, and also expresses the human approach in a most dramatic way:

> Proudly he walks up and down,
> From bough to bough he skips
> On the anag-tree, the ape.
> In his cheek-pouches he sticks
> The sweet fruit of the *manow*.

Father, mother, look at him,
He peers into the distance,
He sees the *bateg'n* fruit,
He grinds them in his fists.
'You, give them to your father!'
His mother shrieks in warning.[9]

The savage does not need to be excused on the grounds that it is natural for him to 'humanise' because apes resemble man in so many ways. When the primitive hunter expresses the actions and motives of apes in human terms he adds to his understanding of them.

I am not suggesting that we should ignore the specific instincts of apes and monkeys and treat them as though they were completely human. The truth probably lies somewhere between the two extremes, but, wherever it lies, we must in the name of reason and understanding *tend* to humanise. We can learn much from the comparatively simple mental and emotional life of monkeys and apes that will help us in our study of the human personality, particularly in respect of children, but this knowledge must grow from a close and continuous relationship with them; it is not enough to adopt a 'scientific' stance, observing them through field-glasses or microscopes, examining their physiology or conducting pathological investigations.

When I emphasise the importance of the animal–human relationship, it does not mean that I condone the animal-lover who plays Chopin to his hedgehog. People have even asked me whether our monkeys play the guitar, and some have taken me seriously when I have answered:

'Not without their music.' But in defence of the animal sentimentalist, is he any less deluded than a lover with his beloved? The erudite old gentleman who treats a simple girl as though she were a female Socrates would do well to remember James Thurber's query: 'Where did you get those lovely blue eyes and that tiny mind?'

To humanise, then, does not mean that we should treat apes as though they were merely backward editions of ourselves; we must also try to communicate with them on their own instinctive level. The difficulties involved are obvious, but the effort is worth making. If, for example, you want to know what is behind the play-bite of a female monkey, bite back. This may lead to a harder bite, which you must also return. Surprisingly enough, you may find that this ends not in a dangerous encounter, but in a collapse of the female in erotic surrender, with much sobbing and chattering of teeth. Respond to this, and you may find yourself locked in a vice-like embrace by two arms, two legs and a twenty-five-inch tail—a situation you will have to accept until her heat subsides. If you think this is unkind, you are greatly mistaken. *You will in fact be guilty of treating the monkey as though she were a human being!* Our healthy and energetic female woolly will not become neurotic or morose, nor will she develop a facial tic or turn to secret drinking. You have only to offer her a few grapes and the whole affair will be forgotten, and if you ask her nicely she will kiss you as a token of her appreciation. It is safe to say that the average human female would not respond to this kind of treatment. It would appear that the food instinct is stronger in the woolly monkey than in the human being (if we exclude the gourmand) and this is one of the many things we should keep in mind whenever we feel disposed to 'humanise' monkey behaviour.

When Samba is naughty, I sometimes threaten her with the cane. Instead of running away, as a child might, she will run towards me and grab hold of the cane to prevent me from using it, at the same time chuckling and shaking her head, expressing a seductive mixture of good humour and defiance which I can best interpret as: 'Oh no you don't, not if I can help it, and anyway, *please* don't, even if you can . . . ha, ha, ha!' If she is in one of her incorrigible moods, I may have occasion to give her a really hard whack, which will cause her to scream with anger; but when the affair is over I have only to say: 'She's a good girl, really, and she's very sorry', and she crawls into my arms and sobs, occasionally opening one eye to see how she is doing. She is totally unafraid, though she knows she cannot rely on my leniency. She is still learning freedom and its disciplines, and in consequence her life is becoming fuller as the years advance, and her character more developed.

Monkeys have the reputation of being impossible as house pets, but we would not think of saying the same of our children, though we know that if they were not disciplined they would create as much havoc in the house as any monkey. Monkeys are trouble simply because they *are* like children. A whole world of do's and don'ts is open to them that a dog cannot enter. One does not say to a dog: 'Stop pulling the baby's hair', 'Don't put your hand in the jam-jar', 'Stop pulling the strings on that guitar', 'Put that cup down carefully'. You cannot acquire a monkey, take it home, put it on the floor and ignore it as you can a dog, because the pyschological and physical machinery of a monkey is so much more developed and adaptable.

If you are unable to provide a monkey with some of the amenities of life that you would give to a child, you have no right to own one. Our monkeys have a centrally heated room of their own that measures sixteen by twelve feet, with ropes, bunks, play-material and an asphalt floor with a gully leading to an outside drain. The entrance door connects with a back zoo-kitchen and our laundry, and the top section of this door (as with most of the doors in our house) consists of plate glass. This provides the monkeys with a view of all kitchen and laundry activities and passing traffic from the front of the house to the back, and it also enables us to see at a glance what is going on inside. A special water-container with a spout protruding through the door provides a constant supply of fresh water, and is refilled from our side. There is access from this room through a hatch to the outside enclosure. The hatch is self-closing by means of a swinging door, and this they open themselves whenever they go out or return. The outside enclosure measures thirty by twenty by fourteen feet. It has a natural grass base, climbing poles, ropes, swings, a revolving wheel, and an outside hut. (It is a good playground for the children also.) The monkeys know best what is good for their own comfort and health, and with plenty of space, fresh air, and warm inside quarters to use as they see fit, they will go out in all weathers, and even play in the snow.

Monkey refuse is collected daily from the inside and outside quarters. The outside enclosure is too large to be fouled by three monkeys; it could in fact accommodate four. Unlike the urine of dogs and cats, which turns grass into straw almost overnight, monkey urine acts on grass as a mild fertiliser. Since monkeys are mainly vegetarians, their droppings are relatively inoffensive compared with those deposited in our garden by neighbours' dogs. This does not stop some people from believing that monkeys stink, and that they are disease-carriers and vermin-ridden. No doubt this belief, which is so far from the truth, is based on visits to the zoo, where a monkey house accommodates fifty or so prisoners who have little else to do but eat, sleep, regurgitate and defecate. This sort of existence, whether in isolation or on a communal basis, enables them to develop a talent for perversions that could only be excelled by men placed under similar conditions. It is often said that animals, by and large, are better off in zoos than in their native haunts. I have no objection to this argument so long as it is made clear that it holds good for one zoo in ten and applies only to certain animals. The London Zoological Gardens, for example, looks after its ants exceedingly well.

I have dwelt at length on the question of suitable conditions for animals because we cannot hope to recognise and understand them as individuals unless we provide them with the conditions which promote health and the fullest possible life. All men lose their identity and become slaves in the galley and the isolation cell; under these conditions, individuality becomes as meaningless as the word democracy in colonial rule. The alternative is not absolute freedom, which is chaos, but disciplined and relative freedom.

The freedom enjoyed by our woolly monkeys would not be possible without discipline. All environments, including natural ones, demand a price for the freedom they offer, and this freedom must be learned. Children's instincts cannot all be gratified, unless we allow them to remain as animals. There is nothing immoral, therefore, about imposing *our freedom* on animals, provided we meet them half way. Monkeys can be taught a great deal within their limits, and they can enjoy the fruits of their instruction no less than children who are corrected as well as loved.

A child should not be brought up with the feeling that the home is full of taboos. That is not discipline, but suppression. There is nothing wrong with the word 'no'— we could hardly get through a minute of the day without it—but we should try to make the word mean 'not that way, but this', 'not here, but there', 'not now, but later'. We say to the infant: 'Yes, pick up the knife, but by the handle. Use the hammer by all means, but not on the windows. Handle the books, but don't tear the pages. Here are the things you can tear and throw about, and here are the things you can't tear and throw about. Use the watering can in the garden, but don't turn it upside down on Father's side of the bed.'

The principle of freedom through knowledge and love,

combined with discipline, must also apply to the animal–
human relationship. A monkey locked up in a cage or
kept on a chain has neither the freedom nor the opportunity to be obedient or disobedient. To this extent it has
a great deal in common with a corpse. (I once saw a Mona
monkey that had never been out of its cage for seven years.
It was in fact a parrot cage, and during its term of im-
prisonment the monkey had grown too large to get
through the entrance door. I presume it died there.)

Samba is allowed to play with any of the children's
toys because she handles them with reasonable care and
has learned not to bite them. Her 'biting instincts' are not
frustrated, since she has plenty of biting and chewing
material in her own quarters, including Max's giant,
granite-like dog-biscuits, which she cracks and eats as
though they were peanuts. Though we have not as yet
managed to convey to her the good sense of being kind,
she can be persuaded (I am not thinking of an order) to
give you something that she does not particularly want,
and this is a step in the right direction.

We treat Samba as though she were a cross between a
good-natured mongoloid child and a sexually mature but
amoral poltergeist. She is five years old. In terms of relative mental and emotional maturity she may be compared
with a human female of sixteen, since the life-span of a
healthy woolly monkey is from twenty to twenty-five
years. But she is a wild animal, even though an incredibly
tame one, and it would be arrogant to imagine one could
fathom all the secrets of her instinctive life. We know some
of these secrets, and we also know that she struggles to

meet us half way. If this is true of Samba the woolly monkey, how much more so would it be of our closer relatives, the chimpanzee and the gorilla?

How can we, and in heaven's name why should we, avoid the tendency to humanise? As I began by saying, if we renounce the human standard of measurement, what standard is left by which to measure anything?

CHAPTER 9

Memories and Tears

WHAT I CHOOSE to call the human approach not only brings us closer to the mind of the animal, but yields its own special kind of knowledge, knowledge which is not quite so unscientific as we have been led to believe. The proposition, for example, that there is in nature a foreshadowing of the moral life of human society is based not on sentimental hope but on the observed facts of animal behaviour.

One of the most illuminating accounts ever given of the animal mind comes from the great naturalist Konrad Lorenz. In his wonderful book *King Solomon's Ring*, he writes: 'When in the course of its evolution, a species of animals develops a weapon which may destroy a fellow-member at one blow, then, in order to survive, it must develop along with the weapon a social inhibition to prevent a usage which could endanger the existence of the species ... I think it a truly magnificent thing that one wolf finds himself unable to bite the proffered neck of the other, but still more so that the other relies upon him for this restraint. Mankind can learn a lesson from this ... I at least have extracted from it a new and deeper understanding of the Gospel which hitherto had awakened in me feelings of strong opposition: "And unto him that smiteth thee on the one cheek offer also the other." A wolf has enlightened me: not so that your enemy may strike you again do you turn the other cheek toward him, but to make him unable to do it.'

Lorenz's observation and interpretation of this aspect of animal behaviour are of tremendous importance, not only because they demonstrate a law of nature—that the submissive gestures and social inhibitions in animal life are part of the self-regulating machinery of evolution—but because they show that these instinctive impulses must be accepted as part of the biological heritage of the human race. In the light of this, the evolution of human morals can be seen as a continuation of the process of nature's machinery for defending the survival of the whole as well as of a particular species.

Lorenz is not suggesting that when the young wolf offers its neck to its adversary we have a situation identical with a human appeal for mercy, or that the older wolf who is inhibited from attacking has adopted the moral position of a man sparing the life of his brother, but he is suggesting that in the behaviour of the wolf we have a demonstration, no matter how primitive or elemental, of love as the victor over aggression and hate.

In stressing the importance of the human approach to animals I do not wish to give the impression that understanding will be advanced by sentimentality. But I do insist that some of the most significant facts about nature and ourselves will never come to light if our interest is confined to the zoological and scientific aspects alone. A man who has a purely scientific or theoretical interest in music will not only fail as a musician, he will never find the true meaning of music. He must also, as if it needs to be said, love music.

To study animals with profit we must also love or learn to love them. This is not to say that all animals can be loved as individuals. We can smile at the idea of a man kissing his alligator good-night. But it is not always appropriate to smile—witness a true story that comes to my mind.

I was working at the Melbourne zoo. Susan, the chimpanzee, had been working with her trainer at Wirth's circus for seven years, having begun her career as a circus performer at two. It is very rare to find a nine-year-old chimpanzee working as a circus animal, for chimpanzees are considered unreliable public performers from the age of five or six onwards. At the age of nine, Susan was as big as any man, and far stronger. Good-natured though she was, Wirth's circus could not afford to take any chances, and so, after many years of active service with the almost constant companionship of Otto her keeper, Susan had been pronounced unreliable and virtually sent to prison.

Some animals are happy in zoos, and some are not. Susan alone in a zoo cage seemed scarcely living. Her movements were reduced to a minimum. Apart from taking a little food and crawling into a corner to sleep on a bed of straw, she spent her days sitting close to the bars of her cage, waiting and watching for Otto. She responded to no one. When Wirth's circus was in Melbourne Otto would visit Susan almost every day, but when the circus moved on she would sometimes have to wait several weeks before she saw him again. I was present at one of these reunions after a long absence, and I have seldom been so moved or saddened as I was on that occasion.

When Otto first appeared, Susan's excitement was terrifying to see. She screamed and whooped, shook the bars of her cage, and jumped about like a mad thing. But when Otto opened the cage door and entered, instead of greeting him Susan retired into a corner and with her back turned towards him sat there in silence. Otto sat down, and began to plead with her in German, softly imploring her to come to him. Several minutes passed before Susan turned her head and looked in his direction. Then she came over to him slowly, her great arms lifted and her lips pouting as she hooted and sobbed, and finally embraced him. Otto played and talked with Susan just as any father would with his own child, and when he left about an hour later I heard Susan's cries from the far end of the zoo long after he had gone. A year later, after I had returned to London, I heard from an Australian friend that Susan had died, presumably of a broken heart.

They say that we cannot have the same feeling about an animal as about a human brother. We may share the experience of enjoying a banana with a monkey or a bunch of carrots with a horse, but we cannot enter the inner world of the instinctive and amoral brute, nor he ours. So they say.

The confusion and error begin, I think, with the fixing of an arbitrary division between unconscious nature and human society, between the amoral and instinctive life of animals and the moral and emotional life of man. The distinction is there, and only a fool would deny it, but many other distinctions of equal importance must be recognised before we can pinpoint in evolution anything so pompous as 'the rise of the moral law in man'.

A certain professor in a television programme on art endeavoured to show that the essential difference between animals and man was that only the latter was able to communicate and share emotional experiences. To illustrate his point, he contrasted a hen bird that accepted dummy eggs as a substitute for real ones with an aeronaut going into orbit. We were supposed to feel detached from, though perhaps amused and a little saddened by the hen, but stimulated and thrilled by the stupendous human reality of the aeronaut. But if we were to contrast the meeting of Susan and Otto in the zoo cage with the rapture enjoyed by the professor over the aeronaut, the verdict could be reversed. As an observer of both events, I at least can sincerely say that I was moved by Susan and Otto, and detached from, though amused and a little saddened by the professor.

I hold, then, that some animals, certainly the higher primates, are capable of individual feelings and possess a certain awareness of their own identity, and that they should therefore be treated as individuals and not simply as representatives of their breed.

It has been said that the loss of an animal friend can be replaced by a substitute, whereas the loss of a human friend leaves a space that remains for ever empty. I am not sure that this is true, for tears are tears; we do not weep in one way for an animal and in another for a human being. The grief we feel at the loss of one of our kind who is dear to us may well cause us to cry out: 'This is different!' But is it so *different*? Is it not instead so very much greater?

When Jess, our five-year-old woolly monkey, died in my arms, I could hardly see him through the tears. This happened two years ago. We still have five woolly monkeys, and Samba is quite as wonderful as Jess. But she will never be a substitute for the Jess who poked his tail at you while standing up and looking in the opposite direction, chuckling like a demon because he wanted a game. Only Jess would run up the side of a door, wait at the top for your signal, and then pancake on to the middle of the bed.

Jess always gave me a kiss if I was holding him too tightly and he wanted to escape. He had a special way of coming very close and peering intently at any little job I was doing about the house, so close that his nose would follow the movements of the screwdriver, yet he never touched it without permission. His eyes would move up and down, concentrating now on the work in hand and now on my face. As he lifted his eyes to my face and then down again to the job I was doing, his expression was always unmistakable: 'What the hell are you up to?' If I swore and cursed, which I have a habit of doing if the job does not go to plan, he would share the experience and express his excitement with a deep-throated 'eelk!' When Jess wanted to eat something from your plate, he always said 'please' with his own special squeak, and he never touched the plate unless you were looking the other way.

Jess was loved, and he deserved to be loved. Ours was a relationship based on trust, affection and the fun of living.

For any animal as highly developed as Jess, there is no substitute. Gavin Maxwell expresses a similar feeling when he tells us about the loss of his otter Mijbil: 'I became, during a year of his constant and violently affectionate companionship, fonder of him than of almost any human being, and to write of him in the past tense makes me feel as desolate as one who has lost an only child . . . and though I now have another otter no whit less friendly and fascinating, there will never be another Mijbil.'[10]

Somewhere down the evolutionary scale the case for replaceability must hold good. But who can fix it, and where? All we can say is that when we consider such creatures as the moth or the ant, in which the individual is completely submerged in the species, a personal relationship from a human point of view is impossible and absurd. This is not to say that these creatures, which belong to nature no less than we do, are unworthy of our admiration, for when we turn our attention from the higher primates with their marked individuality to the mole, the frog, even to the very worms in the earth, love and compassion seem to melt into a simple reverence for nature in the general.

The word that most offends me is 'substitute'. It serves well the language of the critic who says: 'His monkey is a substitute for a previous monkey, or for his failure to establish a satisfactory human relationship.' I am also unsympathetic to the attitude of the self-tortured: 'I shall never have another dog, for no dog could ever be a substitute for Nell. The loss of her is a sadness I cannot bear to think about.'

Images of Jess called up from the past fill me with a great sadness, yet I am conscious that a smile is mixed up in the sadness. These smiling tears express neither an innocent and uncomplicated sorrow, nor morbid self-torture. They are those joyful tears that always come with the memories of those we loved, whether they were animals or humans. We cannot forget what we have truly loved, nor would we wish to. Because of Jess, we gained not only Samba but a greater understanding of Samba, and it is this, not the simple act of suffering, that begets a greater love. It is joy and optimism that conquer pain and suffering. The failure to realise this implies that suffering is the main theme of life, that all comes *out* of it, when in truth all comes *through* it.

Which of us would not prefer to be remembered with a smile? Poor homage for a lively ghost to return to find that those he loved remembered him only with tears. That at any rate is how I feel about a monkey named Jess, and may he never be forgotten.

CHAPTER 10

Primate Intelligence

THE ORDER OF primates includes man, apes, monkeys, lemurs and many other less monkey-like mammals such as galagos and pottos. Although the zoological reasons for grouping them together are mainly anatomical, the higher primates also resemble each other in a particular kind of intelligence and behaviour. Since a definition of primates in strict anatomical and physiological terms cannot indicate the nature of this intelligence and behaviour, we must invent a term of our own. I shall call it 'human-like', but if the bias is disturbing to the scientific disposition I have no objection to calling it 'monkey-like', so long as it is remembered that man, too, is a primate.

There are those who argue that the human-like intelligence of apes and monkeys is not characteristic of their behaviour in the wild, and that it is only displayed in captivity in imitation of human ways. Although this view is a fallacy, as we shall see later, a word first on the 'imitative intelligence' of all primates, including humans.

One can claim that only in the captivity of their social institutions do humans display a higher intelligence than other animals, for where else can any animal display the kind of intelligence that is required for smoking a pipe or riding a bicycle? Under human influence most of the higher mammals, not only monkeys and apes, exhibit a variety of skills that we could hardly expect them to

develop in their natural environment. One is not likely to find a seal balancing a snowball on its nose in the Antarctic.

Indeed one can argue that it is only with the help of human influence that animals can be made to look so stupid and to behave so unintelligently. If breeding lines of apes are going to be established in captivity, let us hope that the animals will not be subjected to some of the worst features of human influence. I am not attracted by the prospect of a proletarian chimpanzee that fetches one's slippers, peels the potatoes and does the washing up, and plays the trombone. If the chimpanzee is to suffer the same fate as the modern show dog, then a few hundred years of domestication should be enough to convert him into a hairy, docile, perfumed sub-moron, who brushes his teeth, uses toilet paper, and accompanies his master on a grouse shoot, himself no mean shot. In short, a chimpanzee that does not creep up behind you and give you a thump on the back when you least expect it is no longer a chimpanzee.

Apes do in fact display a number of human-like characteristics in their natural environment. The South African, Eugène Marais writes: 'It is not only association with human beings that enables apes to evolve their type of intelligence. In many respects our wild troop of baboons showed the same type of intelligence—in a lesser degree— but in its nature there was no difference.'[11]

The picture that Marais gives us of baboon behaviour in the wild, and his case for the psychological evolution of apes and man, throw more light on the unique features of primate behaviour than any evidence we have so far

[113]

considered. He writes: 'Throughout organic nature, birth-pain is coupled with care of the young. Where there is no care of the young there is no birth-pain. In all our observations, no other animal underwent greater birth-pain than the baboon, and mother-love in the baboon reaches a higher stage of development than in any other animal in our country. With the arrival of a new baby a small company gathers together and the baby baboon is handed from one to the other until all have made acquaintance with it. The behaviour of the mother on such occasions is ridiculously human. It is almost as if you could hear her murmur to herself, "Yes, have a good look, you have never seen such a baby before." '[12]

Marais' study also shows that among baboons, apes, and man there is a psychological evolution that tends to free them from the restriction of a limited environment: instinctive knowledge is replaced by individually acquired environmental knowledge, which enables the species to adapt itself to any number of different conditions. For this reason man can live in the Sahara or in the polar regions, just as baboons are found in the mountains of the Cape Peninsula, in the snowy regions of Drakensberg, in the forests as true arboreal animals, and in the Kalahari Desert. This psychological development produces a high degree of individual variation from type, seen at its greatest in the different races of man and in the individual variations within the races. Next to man, these individual variations from type are greater among the baboons and the apes than in any other species of animal. George B. Schaller, who studied the gorilla in its natural habitat, remarks: 'A prominent feature of the intragroup relations was the marked individuality in the behaviour of the animals. An observer soon realises that he is not only studying gorillas as a group or as a specific age and sex class, but also as individuals within that group or class.'[13]

In my view, the human-like behaviour and intelligence that we find in apes, baboons and full monkeys is an expression of a relatively high state of the *evolution of 'individuality' in nature as a whole;* and this individuality is not the sovereign right of primates, be they monkeys or men, but a characteristic that persists, to a lesser extent, in other animal species. The nature of this power, which I propose to call 'creative ability', will be considered in the next chapter.

CHAPTER II

Creative Ability

A NUMBER OF questions arise in common thought, such as: is the elephant more intelligent than the cat, or the monkey than the dog?—questions that zoologists are often unconcerned or unable to answer. They are generally supposed to be unscientific questions on the grounds that all animals are equally intelligent in their own way and for their own purposes. The truth is, they are unscientific in one sense, but in another and equally important sense they are not.

A distinction must be made between the instinctive behaviour of animals and their ability to express and occupy themselves creatively, between what I shall call their instinctive intelligence and their creative intelligence. I believe that by making and supporting this distinction we shall not only be able to answer some of the questions concerning the comparative intelligence of animals, but also gain a clearer picture of the relation between instinctive and creative animal behaviour.

The highest expression of creative ability in the animal kingdom is found in the apes. My own objection to the use of such terms as 'creative intelligence' and 'creative ability' is that they emphasise only the intelligence and the inventive ability of animals, and fail to suggest the nature of their emotional life. Whenever I use these terms, I have in mind the emotional level of the animal as well as its ability to adapt itself to new conditions and its propensity to occupy itself in pursuits which are not dictated by the needs of survival.

The play activity of most animals has a biological significance: kittens, for example, in specialised movements for hunting and prey-catching, are developed and rehearsed. But much of the play-activity in monkeys and apes is due to their craving for variety; it is not determined or driven directly by the needs of survival, though it will obviously be influenced by the latter.

Whenever I speak of the instinctive behaviour of an animal as distinct from its creative ability, I mean those innate movements which express, for example, anger, pleasure, fear and submission; gestures of threat, prey-catching movements, the carriage of body and tail, and the many species-preserving functions which are commonly referred to as instinctive behaviour patterns.

It is possible, of course, to consider animals from the point of view of their aesthetic appeal. Few animals compare with the cat for sheer grace of movement. No matter how much we may admire the functional design of the wart-hog, we must agree that he is not exactly a good-looker: magnificent perhaps, but not beautiful. Whether such aesthetic comparisons are objective, or only express our personal feelings, is irrelevant to the present question. I shall not consider the 'entertainment value' of instinctive actions, such as the grooming and feeding habits of the hamster or the storing mania of the mongoose—rituals that are so appealing and impressive that the observer is tempted to regard them as indications of a high intelligence. Nor shall I compare the instinctive skills of one species with another's, for how could we compare the instinctive intelligence of the beaver with that of the spider without finding ourselves in the ridiculous position of trying to decide whether the beaver displays more intelligence and imagination in the building of a dam than the spider does in spinning its web?

My purpose will be to examine the relation between the behaviour instincts and the creative ability of a given species, and to compare the behaviour characteristics and creative intelligence of various animals one with another. Although the scope for comparative studies of this nature is unlimited, I shall keep mainly to those animals that are well known to us all—the cat, the dog, and the monkey.

* * *

I once heard a man argue that his cat was more intelligent and purposeful than his dog, because the cat persisted on jumping on to the table for food in defiance of repeated threats and even punishment, whereas the dog, once corrected, waited obediently until permission to take the food was given. In this situation the dog's capacity for learning and profiting by experience is clearly greater than that of the cat, from which it follows that the dog is more adaptive as well as more responsive to human influence. It is this very quality in the dog that enables it to act creatively, not only in such simple gestures as the giving of the paw, but in its protective attitude to man and the initiative it displays in conveying its needs and feelings.

Unlike the dog, the cat is not a social animal. Regardless of its domestic history, it has remained a 'wild' creature, not in the sense of being aggressive or savage, but in its self-reliance. The modern domesticated cat is generally considered to be a descendant of the African wild cats, the serval and the caracal, and these beautiful animals, unlike the European wild cats, who are virtually untamable, are well known in zoos for their tractableness. The wild cat is not a social animal, and it stalks its prey alone. Its innate drives and responses conform to an instinctive pattern that resists human influence, and although it has become more docile in the course of domestication, its essential independence and remoteness remain almost unchanged.

The character of the dog, like that of its ancestors the wolf and the jackal, has its roots in the pack instincts of leadership, submission, mutual aid and loyalty. The dog, therefore, has a wider range of instinctive actions and responses to draw upon than the cat, and thus a greater capacity for responding and expressing itself creatively in association with man. The fact that the cat has a shorter domestic history than the dog has little bearing on the point, for even if their domestic histories were equal in length, there can be little doubt that their characters would remain distinct. The essential difference rests in the fact that the domestic cat *continues* to be an independent animal, and the dog *continues* to be a social animal. The personalities of both animals remain tied to the innate behaviour characteristics of their ancestors.

'Individuality' in the cat is in fact considerably less

marked than in the dog; or, to put it another way, dogs are less like each other within their species than cats. I sincerely hope no one will think that I dislike cats. Every animal has its appeal, but for me it is easier to become attached to a dog or a monkey than to a cat. A close relationship with a cat is a one-way affair. You may feel close, but the cat will not.

The dependence of the dog on its master arises out of the instinctive loyalty of the wild dog to the pack-leader. Because of this 'transference' in the man-dog relationship, the development of the young dog is sometimes arrested and kept at the infantile stage. Although the extreme 'childishness' observable in some dogs must be regarded as a character defect, it must also be seen as the reverse side of a trait that is positive, i.e. a capacity for loyalty and affection of a very high order. In dogs fawning is no indication of healthy obedience, and the extreme pleasure derived from petting cannot be regarded as an expression of real affection, yet it would be quite wrong to attribute these traits to an inherent weakness in the character of dogs in general. It cannot be claimed as a comparative virtue that this behaviour is uncharacteristic of the cat, for the very reason that the cat is by nature resistant or incapable of the kind of affection and loyalty that is characteristic of the dog. It is easier to corrupt a sensitive man than an insensitive one, but this does not mean that the latter has a stronger and a larger character, any more than the absence of fear presupposes courage. The mental and emotional life of the house dog, the wolf and the wild dog functions on a more evolved or higher level of instinctive behaviour than that of the cat, which is precisely why the dog is more responsive and creative in his relationship with man. I have never heard of a guard cat, though I understand that relatively tame and well-fed lions have been known to roam the estates of Eastern potentates.

It is because some animals within the higher mammalian groups exhibit distinct and highly individual characteristics that we call them 'personalities'. When we study those animals that represent earlier and more primitive stages in evolution, such as the opossum and the koala, we find one member of the species almost identical in behaviour and appearance with another. If we refer to the koala as a 'personality', it is the 'personality' of the species that we have in mind, and not the individual koala. (To my prejudiced eye they are all the same, though they do come in different sizes.) A few words on the koala 'himself' will, I think, throw this into relief.

The koala has perhaps suffered more indignity and persecution from human hands than any other animal in nature. This innocent creature, relic of prehistory and prototype of the teddy-bear, has become the world's 'most adorable creature', and so great is his popularity with tourists that some have declared that he alone made their visit worth while. Apart from being an easy target for 'sportsmen' to shoot and for others to throw stones at, nearly nine million of these defenceless little creatures were killed by hunters for their fur between 1920 and 1928. Through the protection of reserves, the koala today is increasing in numbers, and can no longer be hunted, exploited, or kept in captivity. He cannot survive in captivity unless placed in conditions identical with those of his own habitat, which is why you are not likely to see one at the zoo. He lives on the leaves of one type of eucalyptus tree, and any change of diet gives him fatal indigestion. When I was at the Melbourne zoo a fresh supply of eucalyptus leaves arrived every day at the koala enclosure, yet the mortality rate remained high.

The koala, of course, is an Australian marsupial and not a bear. He may resemble the teddy-bear, he may even have inspired the teddy-bear, but in appearance, behaviour and temperament he is nothing like a bear. As for his cuddlesome appeal, he must be handled with extreme care, for he bites, unpredictably and without warning, and his claws are capable of inflicting a serious wound—as anyone who has been rash enough to climb a eucalyptus tree to catch a koala will know. In the mating season the call-cries of the koala can be heard echoing through the Australian bush. The sound, which resembles the noise of a saw cutting through iron, is as prehistoric as the koala's own anatomy. He is said to wear a smile, but this is due to the shape of his muzzle, for his face, like that of the South American sloth, is permanently innocent of any kind of expression. He is not an emotional animal.

I love the koala as a species, as a manifestation of nature, but communication between me and the individual koala is restricted to one situation. Up a tree in the Australian bush, a picture of vegetative bliss, he looks down at me, languidly and vacantly, while I, at the foot of the tree, look up at him and think how much better the tree looks with him in it—two creatures on the one earth, each gazing shortsightedly at the other, with no enmity whatever, yet neither feeling the slightest desire to shake hands or say hello. All one can do is to give the tree an affectionate pat and wander on to another part of the forest. Nevertheless, it is a wonderful experience to walk through the reserves and see these quaint toy-like creatures clinging to the branches of the eucalyptus tree, serene and detached, as though happy in the knowledge that evolution has passed them by.

If I have been unkind to the individual koala, it has only been with the object of making my point: that as individuality within the species decreases, so does the scope for communication between the animal and the human observer, whether he be a friend, an investigator, or both. That is why even the strongest attachment to an animal can never give expression to the deepest and most urgent needs of man. Yet who is to decide where respect and reverence should end, and love begin? Can the critic who thinks we should confine our 'specifically human' feelings—whatever they are supposed to be—to members of our own species, tell us where we should draw the line—at the Tasmanian aborigine, the Neanderthaler, the gorilla, the woolly monkey, the dog? I draw mine somewhere on the level of dog–seal–raven, but this is a wholly subjective approach, and I would not enjoy the task of justifying it on any but personal grounds.

Just as the dog has a wider range of instinctive social responses to draw upon than the cat, so has the monkey compared with the dog. It is more difficult to assess the monkey's comparative power of understanding human language because he is by nature less obedient than the dog. The monkey that lives under ideal conditions with a human family, such as most dogs enjoy, is frequently preoccupied and gives one the impression that he is not listening or does not understand what is being said to him. We know that the dog is more loyal, more dedicated to his master and the family, that he has a smaller life of his own and that there are all manner of things he can do that a monkey couldn't—I cannot see a monkey competing with a working sheepdog or with a fox terrier when it comes to catching a rat. But if we are to measure animals in terms of their instinctive skills and their usefulness to man, we shall have to bring the cow, the silkworm and a host of other creatures into the picture, and the object of this study will be lost. The special skills which are inseparable from the behaviour instincts of the various species must not be confused with the ability of animals to learn new techniques and occupy themselves creatively in new conditions. If anyone were to ask me why I like monkeys in particular, the best short answer I could give would be: 'Because they laugh, sigh, yawn, burp, snort, sneeze, scratch, sniff, squeak, cry, sob, and gurgle, and pick their noses.'

The stronger individuality and inventiveness of the monkey compared with the dog becomes apparent when both animals are left to occupy themselves during what, from their point of view, may be described as a dull evening at home. Max is lying on a couch in the lounge, his eyes turned and fixed on me. He can go out into the garden, but this evidently does not appeal to him. He can grunt, sigh, close his eyes or keep them open, go to sleep and dream, or stay awake. He can look at me and whine (Alsatians are extremely vocal), because he feels like a game, or wants to be taken out, or would like me to tell him what he wants to do. He may lift his head suddenly, and, alert and erect, give a low rumbling growl because a small sound outside the house has displeased him. It is a situation that often induces my wife to say: 'What a pity Max can't read.'

We don't really feel sorry for Max. Life could be better for him; but it could be better for all of us. He has the freedom of large front and back gardens that surround the house, he is taken out regularly to the woods and fields near by, and he is often tired out from a day's battle with two infant boys and the woolly monkey Jimmy, all of whom help to make his life more difficult as well as more interesting. If he really wants a game he knows where to find an old shoe, and that I usually oblige when he drops it at my feet.

Max prefers the cool air coming through the open door, but he will close it if we ask him to. We don't, because when he stands up on his hind legs and gives the door the full benefit of his one hundred and five pounds, it shuts with a mighty bang and wakes up the children. Apart from the door-closing act, which is extremely useful, we have taught him nothing except 'heel', 'off', and similar disciplines. But he has learned a number of tricks of his own making, most of them inspired by coping with the monkeys and the children.

So there he lies, resting or waiting, we can never be sure which, a study in expectation, his eyebrows wrinkled in disappointment, but thankful at least that baby Daniel has gone to bed and is not crawling all over his belly. What to do? Well, he's not a greedy dog; the main meal will arrive later, and there are always biscuits and bones and water in the zoo-kitchen. He therefore indulges in the greatest pastime known to dogs: he does nothing.

Now look at Samba. Like Max, she is not feeling very energetic, for she has spent most of the day chasing Liz in the outside enclosure. She has just topped off an evening meal with another apple, two shortcake biscuits, one of the baby's rusks, a piece of bacon she found on the floor, some grapes and a cup of tea, but any moment now she will begin to feel peckish. The clock chimes and she frowns as she turns her head, saying 'yook, yook' very softly, which means great displeasure. She hates the clock, especially when it chimes, because we will not allow her to open the back of it and investigate the mystery inside. Her eyes rest on a fruit-bowl on the sideboard that contains some nuts. She slides down from my lap, and although on her way over she herself displays no interest whatever in one of the children's toys, her tail does, as if it had said to itself: 'We might as well take this along too; you never can tell.'

Arriving at the sideboard, the toy still held in her tail, Samba opens a door that swings out, climbs on to it and sits there, looking at the bowl of nuts. Lifting one hand tentatively, she turns her head, and with the hand poised over the bowl pauses for a few moments to see whether

I am watching. I look at her, expressionless and silent. She says 'eelk', this time a tiny, distant, high-pitched eelk which I have learned to interpret as 'All is well, is it, I hope?' I may say: 'Yes, Samba, help yourself.' If I say nothing, she will anyway. She then comes over to me, climbs up and drops the nuts in my lap, and waits for my approval. If I ignore her, she picks up my hand, the one with no cigarette in it, and places it on the nuts. And the toy, which has remained in the grasp of her prehensile tail all the while, will also be dropped on to my lap along with the nuts. If I now say in a whispering voice: 'You've been a very naughty girl', she will lift up her arm and cover her eyes with her hand and sob.

The point I have tried to make here is that so much was going on about so little, that the journey from my lap to the bowl of nuts and back again was a study in cunning and forethought, resolved in an enchanting mixture of affection and 'crocodile tears'.

*　　*　　*

There is a danger of treating behaviour instincts as though they were simply a blockage to new knowledge and techniques, when in fact they are *also* the ground or basic pattern on which they can be developed. That is why monkeys—who have no domestic history—are none the less more intelligent and emotionally expressive than dogs: they possess a more varied range of instinctive movements to draw upon. The instincts of the wombat are a greater impediment to the expression of inventive intelligence than are the instincts of the cat, but the instinctive behaviour of the wombat is not in itself an impediment, as might be proved should anyone be tempted to encourage this humble creature to develop whatever creative ability it may possess. A similar comparison can be made of the cat in relation to the dog, of the dog to the monkey, the monkey to the ape, and the ape to man.

Granted that the dog has no prehensile tail, no hands, and no muscles capable of expressing the range of feeling one sees in the face of the woolly monkey; but if this point is pressed to its logical end, we shall find ourselves defending the spider on the grounds that, given the physical and psychological machinery of the primate man, it could play the lute. Nevertheless, the mental and emotional life of the dog or the undomesticated wolf, who belong to the order of canidae, is immeasurably higher and closer to the human standard than that of the lemur and the half-monkeys in the lower order of primates.

In conclusion, it seems to me that there is an evolution of individuality at work in nature, and with it a development of creative ability that enables animals to rely more on the learning of new techniques and less on instincts that are inborn, a development in fact towards *social culture*, where individuality finds its highest expression, for better or for worse.

CHAPTER 12

Apes and Art

WHEN SAMBA SITS on my lap and peers into my face, she never fails to notice a pimple that sometimes lights up the end of my nose. She shows no interest in the rest of the nose, and gives all her attention to that particular area. Samba has an instinctive preference for certain colours, patterns, and shapes. An enlarged nose, coloured red and with a dot in the middle, is more interesting for her than a normal one.

Professor Bernhard Rensch has shown that birds, as well as monkeys, have a preference for certain colours and symmetrical patterns. His preference tests are valuable because they confirm that an instinct for organisation, symmetry and rhythm is rooted in the very heart of life. Dr Desmond Morris, however, takes us a step further. In his book *The Biology of Art* he maintains that apes are able to enjoy aesthetic creation with abstract shapes and patterns, and that the ape and modern man have much the same reason for painting pictures.

Because apes are our next of kin we would expect to find the instinct for organisation and design stronger in them than in other animals; but only in man is this instinct raised to the power of aesthetic intuition and expression. Konrad Lorenz has indicated that in nature there is a foreshadowing of the moral life of man;[14] but when he refers to the instinctive inhibitions that prevent a wolf from using his weapons against another of his own kind, he does not mean that the wolf is a moral philosopher; the wolf has no moral consciousness, just as the infant and the ape have no artistic intuition.

My experience with children and chimpanzees has taught me to love and wonder at their naïveté, their charm, and the logic that underlies all their instinctive impulses. They both crave variety, though every new act they perform will be repeated until interest wanes. For example, when an infant first grasps the idea of a circle he will move the pencil round and round, superimposing one circle upon another very rapidly, making several circular movements before stopping. This repetition is driven by the desire for action and movement. The infant is not interested in the result, no matter whether the result is an 'aesthetic fact' or a hole torn in the paper. He may in fact look at you and laugh with delight while still drawing the circle. But he will not stop, as though to say: 'Behold! I have drawn a circle!' He does not finish a drawing; he stops drawing, or he continues to make more circles, or runs the circles into loops or fans, or obliterates the whole with more scribbling, or stops when the paper is fully covered, or when interest lags, or when he wants his napkin changed.

An animal that can throw sticks, smoke a pipe, catch a ball and return it and point with the finger at new objects, will display a similar initiative and dexterity in anything it does, whether it be drawing with a pencil or playing with Plasticine. We do not regard the chimpanzee as a fundamentalist in the first principles of mathematics because he can count up to seven, and it is equally absurd to present him as an artist capable of pure aesthetic creation with abstract colour patterns because he daubs as intelligently as a child of two. Apes are intelligent, and they have a sense of humour. That makes them wonderful enough. Many years ago at the Melbourne zoo a keeper accidentally left a can of paint in the cage of Tang the orang-utan. When he returned, Tang had painted the rest of the cage, the whole floor, and himself as well. He was covered with paint from head to foot, and it was months before it wore off.

In Dr Morris's book an account is given of a chimpanzee who became sexually excited when painting. Monkeys and apes, like children, often become sexually stimulated by a new interest or game, yet Dr Morris is sufficiently intrigued by this healthy reaction to suggest that it might be an aberrant response worthy of further investigation. Our woolly monkey Pepi often sat on the table of our zoo kitchen while I prepared the monkey food, and the extent to which he was sexually excited by the prospects of a bowl of rice pudding was a delight to see. On these occasions my wife used to say: 'Pepi's resting his chin on his microphone again!' Infant boys often have erections during bath-time, and children will sometimes urinate involuntarily when they are over-excited or bursting with enthusiasm because of a new interest.

There is no special significance in the fact that chimpanzees are completely absorbed by their painting without the usual rewards of food that are given during intelligence tests. Many tests of intelligence other than painting require no material reward, for the simple reason that there are two kinds of intelligence tests: those that are interesting for the animal, and those that are not.

Samba will unscrew a lid from a jar, turn a door-handle, pick up a cup and drink from it and put it down again so that it will not tip over, catch a ball, and perform many other little operations that can be regarded as intelligence tests. She is not absorbed by any of these commonplace operations, and she will not open a door unless she wants to enter the room, unscrew a lid unless the jar contains some delicacy, or pick up a cup unless she wants to drink. But if you give her a new toy, or even an old one in which she has a special interest, she becomes absorbed and nothing within reason can distract her attention from it. She often busies herself with a toy telephone receiver— the property of our infant son—which has a moving dial that makes a little bell-like tinkle. Most of her time is spent in trying to take everything apart; the earpiece must be unscrewed, the lead detached, the dial removed. Her concentrated occupation with simple mechanical gadgets is for its own sake; there is no question of a reward. Similarly, if Samba is given a piece of rope that is tied in several knots, she will give herself over entirely to unravelling it for no other reason than that she enjoys doing it. If all this is so of a woolly monkey, whose intelligence and initiative are considerably less than a chimpanzee's, it is only to be expected that chimpanzees will become absorbed in a variety of play activities that bring no material reward, and that painting will be only one among many.

The hand of the higher primates is designed to perform

a number of complex rhythmical movements, and in a welter of pencil-scribbling and paint-daubing it is unable to avoid making horizontal, vertical and diagonal lines, loops and curves, just as a chimpanzee sitting at the piano will sometimes play major and minor thirds by accident, and even triads, simply because he has a hand action and fingers that fall naturally on to these harmonic combinations. The chimpanzee interests himself with the mechanical action of the keyboard and with the different sounds he is able to make. It can be said that he is enjoying himself, but it cannot be said that he is creating music, that he is aware of music, or that he is expressing himself musically.

If you give a guitar to a chimpanzee, once the relation between cause and effect is grasped (between the touching of the strings and the sound it makes, as with the moving of the pencil and the marks that appear on the paper), a number of interesting things begin to happen. Thumping the strings with the open hand makes a drum-like sound. Dragging the nails of all the fingers swiftly and strongly across the strings near the bridge-piece gives a fair imitation of the Flamenco style of playing. Over a period of time the chimpanzee makes a number of exciting discoveries, and experiments with a variety of attacks on different strings. We are impressed by his inventive intelligence and imitative ability, but we do not regard his spontaneous efforts as basic patterns in 'pure music-making'!

There can be no objection to regarding the play-instinct as a form of self-expression. But art is more than self-expression; it is as wrong to find the elements of it in the scribbling of a chimpanzee as to seek music in the singing of birds or the call-cries of monkeys. The birds make delightful sounds, but not *music*. The great musicologist, Curt Sachs, has said: 'The mammals, man's closest relatives, may whine and whistle, bark and roar; the ape, his nearest cousin, grunts and coughs. There is no singing among man's next of kin.'[15]

The belief that apes have artistic potentialities has its counterpart in the Darwinian hypothesis that apes are able to produce and respond to musical tones. Darwin writes: 'Primeval man probably first used his voice in producing true musical cadences, that is in singing, as do some of the gibbon-apes at the present day . . . and we may conclude that this power would have been especially exerted during the courtship of the sexes.'[16]

In the field studies of trained observers there is no evidence that apes utter a sex-call, least of all a 'song of love', during a preliminary stage of their mating. Schaller, in his study of the mountain gorilla, noted a staccato cry, and loud growls and grunts which occurred during copulation, but he heard no cries that could be connected with sexual overtures or 'courtship'. The initiation of gorilla sexual behaviour is expressed by strutting displays on the part of the male, or by receptive females presenting themselves. I have been able to study a large range of call-cries in our own woolly monkey community, but none of these is connected with mating behaviour during initiation or copulation. They are signal calls, expressing 'All is well', 'Danger', and variants of these. Unlike the copulation sounds, which consist of sighs, sobs, grunts and squeaks, and are anything but musical, their call-cries are among some of the most beautiful sounds I have ever heard in nature.

Darwin's approach to the origins of music is so naïve that it is difficult to take some of his conclusions seriously. Take, for example, the following quotation: 'Judging from the hideous ornaments and equally hideous music admired by most savages, it might be argued that their aesthetic faculty was not so highly developed as in birds.'[17] Darwin evidently preferred the chirruping of canaries to the beautiful chants and dynamic rhythms of Australian aboriginal music, and believed that apes and early man yodelled for their mates. He refused to be influenced by his contemporaries— Schoolcraft, Tyler, Rowbotham, and Morgan—who already knew that mating and courtship behaviour (not to be confused with fertility rituals) played no part in the music and ritual of the most primitive races. There are, of course, biological links between the sounds and rhythmic behaviour of animals and the music and dancing of primitive man, but Darwin, like modern writers who have resurrected his fictions, had a poor ear for music and no understanding of the nature of its origins.

In informal language we may say that gibbons sing and that chimpanzees dance, but we do not mean that gibbons sing music, or that chimpanzees dance to or because of rhythm. If they dance rhythmically it is because they find it extremely difficult to jump up and down unrhythmically, just as we would find it difficult to breathe irregularly.

I have discussed the question of chimpanzee 'dancing' with many circus trainers, and they all agree that the chimpanzee has no real sense of rhythm. This is the opinion of the famous chimpanzee trainer Rudi Lenz. His chimpanzees enjoy themselves in their 'jazz band' act. They are excited and stimulated by the music, and each performer will stamp his feet, beat a drum, and hit a cymbal with wild enthusiasm. But Lenz insists that not one of them, as an individual or in the group, has ever displayed a rhythmical ability remotely connected with keeping time to music.

Almost every specialist in ape behaviour has commented on the alleged 'rhythmic dancing' of chimpanzees both in the wild and in captivity. Even trained investigators like Köhler and Yerkes have claimed that chimpanzees are able to dance 'in time to music,' but they produce no evidence to support these conclusions. My own observations and tests indicate that chimpanzees will exhibit rhythmic action in their intimidation displays, and also when they are frightened or excited. These displays consist of much foot-stamping and 'drumming', jumping up and down, rocking from foot to foot and swaying rhythmically. A parrot on its perch will also rock and sway in rhythm. It would be an eccentric bird that did otherwise. The sustained repetition of any action in the animal world would not be possible without a certain amount of regularity, but the rhythm implicit in such regularity is determined by motor impulse and not by a sensuous and rhythmic feeling in the psychic life of the animal.

Though we cannot credit animals with either a musical

or rhythmic sense, an instinctive rhythm is nevertheless deeply rooted in the heart of nature; in breathing, walking, the act of procreation, the dripping of water, the flapping of a bird's wings. It has even been suggested that the repeated syllables of infant babble are to some extent influenced by the sounds of the heart-beat first heard by the embryo in the mother's womb.

The rhythmic sounds of nature are impressive and mysterious, and they belong to a different order of sound to the warbling of birds and the cries of monkeys and apes. The historian of music John Rowbotham writes: 'There is a sound which is fraught with mystery, a sound which is Nature's magic, for by it dumb things can speak . . . When that strange and curious man first struck together his two pieces of wood, he had other aims than his own delight in sensuous sound; he was trying to create something that had mystified him. That something was rhythmic sound—on which roots the whole art of music.'[18]

Apes can be puzzled and intrigued, and they have a sense of fear, but they have no sense of mystery, and they have no sense of rhythm. Man was the first animal to discover rhythm and become aware of the mystery of rhythmic sound. He danced this rhythm to a stage of rhythmic trance in his fear and worship of the unknown, unseen forces of nature. When he added his own speech sounds as well as the emotive cries of his primate ancestors to rhythmic action and chanting in his magic ritual, he was fashioning the true beginnings of music and dancing as art.

In his fertility-ritual and hunting-dances and in his cave paintings, Palaeolithic man sought a magic control of the mysterious processes of birth and generation. Like his primate ancestors he was ignorant of these processes but unlike them he was moved and disturbed by the 'knowledge' of mystery, by a respect and a fear of forces he could not understand.

The ape is aware of what he sees and he knows well where to find his food. He is alert to the dangers of the forest and skilled in avoiding them. He is aware of disease and knows that it brings pain. He is frightened by tropical storms and by strange sounds that come from objects and places that he cannot see. Like the first men, he does not know why the food he gathers must grow, and why it is sometimes scarce, nor why the snake is poisonous, the night cold, or the sun warm. Like the mother baboon who carries her dead baby around with her while it decomposes in her arms, the ape is distressed by the fact that his mate does not behave as though she were alive, *but he does not know that she is dead.*

Neanderthaler knew, doomed though he was to extinction. He buried the bodies and the bones of his dead and coloured them with red ochre. Red is the colour of life and health, and since shells and ornaments of bone and ivory were also deposited in the graves, it is clear that Neanderthaler had some kind of belief in the supernatural. He survived the Ice Age of the late Pleistocene period. He made flake tools, a flint-tipped spear, hunted the rhinoceros, and taught his skills to his children, which required speech and discipline[19]. No doubt Neanderthaler was as much in awe of nature, and danced and sang no less than the men who came after him.

The supreme difference between the ape mind and the mind of man consists in this: man is *aware* of what he cannot explain; he is conscious of mystery, and not simply mystified. He must explain and express the unknown and the unseen, for there reside the powers which control his life. This is the key to the religious, moral, and artistic life of the first men, and that is why, in my view, the rhythmic action, vocalising, and play-activity of apes has only a *pathogenic* link with the origins of human art.

CHAPTER 13

Concrete and Straw

ANYONE WHO HAS SEEN the gorilla Guy at the London zoo will agree that he is a magnificent specimen. Guy, who weighs more than four hundred pounds, spends most of his day sitting on concrete. As I write, he has already served seventeen years of a life sentence, a sentence with no privileges, no comrades, and no materials for work or play. What does he do all day? He sits and he regurgitates.

I wish to make a plea for Guy, and in doing so I have in mind not only Guy but all those monkeys and apes who are imprisoned in zoo cages under appalling conditions. My object will be to show that the lot of the isolated zoo gorilla is a shameful one; that the captive gorilla mother and her infant are little better off; that the remedy is not to abolish gorillas from zoos and look at them through field-glasses in the national parks and conservation areas; and, finally, that a practical solution does exist, that will provide for the welfare of the gorilla in captivity, advance the enjoyment of the spectator, and present a unique opportunity for scientists to study the social behaviour of the gorilla in conditions mid-way between those of a zoo and his natural habitat.

The most a gorilla or a chimpanzee can hope for in the average zoo is food, shelter, straw, and, if he is lucky, a rubber tyre. Monkeys, who are far more active than gorillas, are even less fortunate. It is an unhappy irony that monkeys and apes, who are the most human-like of all the animals, suffer the poorest conditions in captivity in relation to their needs and habits. By comparison, the fish in the aquaria and the goats in their paddocks move with the freedom and style of aristocrats.

A gorilla mother likes to put her infant on the ground at regular intervals and leave it unattended, for this encourages it to crawl. At the Basle zoo the infant gorilla Goma crawled when she was placed on a carpet, but she would not crawl on the cement floor of a cage. The mother also releases her hold to develop the infant's ability to grip, and in the event of a mishap catches the falling infant in her hands. What is not always appreciated is that although an accident would not matter if it occurred in the natural environment of the gorilla, among long grass, tangled foliage, or on moss-covered earth, it would be extremely dangerous on a concrete floor.

The gorilla resembles man in that certain instincts require the example of the social group in order to function properly. This may account for the failure of Achilla at the Basle zoo to give proper attention to her first baby, Goma. The gorilla mother offers her young for inspection and approval to trusted members of the family group, and it is natural for her to make this gesture to her keeper in a zoo. When Achilla offered her baby to the director of the Basle zoo, she tried to push it under the iron grill of her cage and had to be prevented from unintentionally harming it. The zoo cage, with its cement floor, iron bars, and restricted space—the inside and outside cells of Guy's quarters each measure approximately sixteen by fourteen feet—is a threat to the welfare of the mother and her infant.

The most stable human relationship would break down under the strain imposed on parent gorillas in a zoo cage, and it is no wonder that the Basle and Washington zoos found it necessary to separate the male parent from the mother and baby. Deprived of their natural habitat as well as the influence of the family group, and with no means of escape from a temperamental and interfering father, the captive gorilla family is in an intolerable situation. Sedatives, vitamin preparations, pregnancy tranquillisers, stimulants, comprehensive tables and diagrams of dentitions and post-natal weight graphs—all the resources of modern medical science are at the disposal of the gorilla mother, while she lives with a baby on a few square feet of concrete.

Sober estimates of the gorilla's life-span in the wild agree that it is somewhere between thirty and forty years, yet in the London Zoological Society *Yearbook* the average life-span of gorillas in the London zoo is shown as ten years. We can only hope that Guy will not suffer the fate of Eseka at the Berlin zoo, who reached full maturity and weighed two hundred and twenty-five pounds, then fell into a mysterious decline and died from general debility. The physicians and veterinary surgeons who examined her could find no trace of disease. An autopsy was carried out, but no organ showed any sign of morbidity. Eseka just faded away.

Despite all I have said, I still believe that zoos are necessary institutions, and that the arguments directed against them in principle are hardly worth examination. Some animals enjoy more freedom in zoos than in their wild state. Freedom is a peculiar word. Freedom from what, and to do what? Freedom for the gorilla to return to what is left of its native haunts, to catch a virus disease that often destroys whole families of them in a matter of weeks, or to be hunted and killed for its meat by natives? Freedom for a vast number of African animals to return to nature reserves determined by the needs of man, barren and infertile areas which have no economic, industrial, or agricultural value for the human invader?

The real problem for the national parks and wild life organisations is to make the conservation areas permanent, and to see that they are properly planned and controlled. Whatever happens in the future, it is obvious that the zoos can and must play a vital part in the preservation of wild life. They have in fact already done so, for a number of animals already extinct in the wild, such as the European bison and the Mongolian wild horse, are breeding well in captivity. There are even those who believe that this responsibility will one day be taken over entirely by the zoos. I believe that something is needed between the over-populated zoo metropolis and the great nature reserves. I see a great future for the small zoo-park or sanctuary, specialising in certain species and set in a few acres of natural woodland.

An acre of woodland would not be fouled by a group of five gorillas. The grasses would certainly survive, and so would the trees if protected by steel netting to a trunk height of ten feet. Gorillas are mainly terrestrial, and though they readily climb around in trees, they are not likely to be destructive when their food is provided for them. I hope one day to enclose an acre of woodland for gorillas in my own sanctuary. There is no reason why a successful breeding line of gorillas should not be established for the first time in a British sanctuary, and I would welcome the opportunity of working with any interested person or wild life organisation to that end.

The English climate is no obstacle; our woolly monkeys play in the snow, and the chimpanzees on their island at the Chester zoo have thrived during the severest of English winters. In the Virunga volcanoes area, gorillas frequent the mountain forests at altitudes of over 13,000 feet, where the temperature falls to near freezing point at night. It is a common fallacy that all tropical animals require a tropical climate. Most of them are in fact distressed by the heat, and like ourselves would much prefer to live on the French Riviera.

*   *   *

Next time you go to the zoo, stand in front of the gorilla and look deep into his eyes; notice how they flash from side to side, feel their intensity when they rest on you, and marvel not only at the great primaeval force that lurks behind them, and their compelling beauty, but at their human appeal—an appeal that fills me with a deep sense of shame as well as wonder.

REFERENCES IN TEXT

1. *The River Amazon From Its Sources to the Sea,* Paul Fountain. London, Constable & Co., 1914

2. *A Narrative of Travels on the Amazon and Rio Negro,* Alfred Russel Wallace. London, Ward, Lock & Co., 1853

3. *A Journey Across South America,* Paul Marcoy. Translated by E. Rich. London, Blackie & Son, 1873

4. *Recollections of an Ill-Fated Expedition to the Headwaters of the Madeira River in Brazil,* N. B. Craig. London, Lippincott, 1907

5. *The River Amazon From Its Sources to the Sea,* Paul Fountain. London, Constable & Co., 1914

6. *The Naturalist in Nicaragua,* Thomas Belt. London, John Murray, 1874

7. *Mammals of Amazonia,* Elaido da Cruz. Rio de Janeiro, 1945

8. *The Rivers Ran East,* Leonard Clark. London, Hutchinson, 1954

9. *Cenalora* (Leben, Glaube, Tanz und Theater der Urvolker), Oskar Eberle. Freiburg, Olten, 1955

10. *Ring of Bright Water,* Gavin Maxwell. London, Longmans, Green, 1960

11. *My Friends the Baboons*, Eugène Marais. London, Methuen, 1939

12. *Ibid.*

13. *The Mountain Gorilla*, George Schaller. Chicago and London, University of Chicago Press, 1963

14. *King Solomon's Ring*, Konrad Lorenz. Translated by Marjorie Kerr Wilson. London, Methuen, 1952

15. *The Rise of Music in the Ancient World, East and West*, Curt Sachs. London, J. M. Dent & Sons, 1944

16. *The Descent of Man*, Charles Darwin. London, John Murray, 1871

17. *Ibid.*

18. *A History of Music*, John F. Rowbotham. London, Trübner & Co., 1885–87

19. *The Origin of Races*, Carleton S. Coon. London, Jonathan Cape, 1963

DATE DUE

30 505 JOSTEN'S